THE CRACKWALKER

Also by Judith Thompson

THE CRACKWALKER
JUDITH THOMPSON

PLAYWRIGHTS CANADA PRESS
TORONTO

PLAYWRIGHTS CANADA PRESS
The Canadian Drama Publisher
215 Spadina Ave., Suite 230, Toronto, ON Canada M5T 2C7
phone 416.703.0013 fax 416.408.3402
orders@playwrightscanada.com • www.playwrightscanada.com

Playwrights Canada Press acknowledges the financial support of the Government of Canada through the Canada Book Fund and the Canada Council for the Arts, and of the Province of Ontario through the Ontario Arts Council and the Ontario Media Development Corporation for our publishing activities.

 Canada Council Conseil des Arts
for the Arts du Canada

 ONTARIO ARTS COUNCIL
CONSEIL DES ARTS DE L'ONTARIO

 Canadä Ontario
Ontario Media Development Corporation

Cover painting *Down the Lido* by Helen Healy, photographed by
Steve McKinley
Cover and type design by Blake Sproule

LIBRARY AND ARCHIVES CANADA CATALOGUING IN PUBLICATION
Thompson, Judith, 1954-
The crackwalker / Judith Thompson. -- 2nd ed.

A play.
ISBN 978-0-88754-931-1

I. Title.

PS8589.H4883C73 2010   C812'.54   C2010-904908-X

First edition: September 2003
Second edition: September 2010
Printed and bound in Canada by Gauvin Press, Gatineau

This play is dedicated to the memory of my father.

The Crackwalker Thirty Years Later

In April 1979, in Montreal, in my third year at the National Theatre School, I found myself alone on a spring Sunday. Everybody was away or busy, and being twenty-four years old, I was feeling quite desperate.

And so I began *The Crackwalker*. I pulled out my roommate's old typewriter, and just began tapping away.

I didn't really know I was writing a play, but knew I had a wonderful voice—the voice of Theresa, remembered from recent experiences on the streets of Kingston. As I wrote, I decided I would give Teresa a friend, Sandy, loosely basing her on a waitress I had worked with at Nikos deli in Kingston, before I got fired for almost hilarious incompetence. She was rail thin, and often arrived with bruises, but she was a crackerjack waitress. I was healthy and plump, and the worst waitress ever. I didn't even understand what the bruises meant, but they haunted me, and that glimpse into another world became the character of Sandy. As I wrote, I felt like I was a child playing with dolls; the two females needed boyfriends, I thought, so I brought in Alan and Joe. And the characters just spilled out onto the page, virtually creating themselves. When I think about it, I had been given full permission to let my characters take over me by the late Pierre LeFevre, the most brilliant and inspiring theatre teacher I have ever had—he encouraged a kind of channelling with the masks, or a surrender of the public-constructed self to the character that emerged from the mask, and I found myself doing this as I wrote. As the play took shape I was quite surprised by what came out, especially at the climax—I had not planned to write about the death of a baby, but it was as if that story, which was true, insisted upon being told. The summer before, I had lucked into a job with the Ministry of Community and Social Services, teaching life skills to the permanently unemployable of Kingston. Mainly, I taught a motley crew of enchanting hard-luck characters that underwear went in the drawer, not the freezer, and that Coke and chips was not a healthy dinner, and that it was not cool to pull a knife on someone because they took a drag off your cigarette. Also, I tried to teach reading and writing. And grocery shopping and budgeting. Theresa, the character I created in *The Crackwalker*, was loosely based on a Theresa who was my most delightful client that summer—I had the privilege of teaching her reading and writing and just hanging out with her, going to Zal Yanovsky's first café and drinking exotic drinks like mango juice, crazy for Kingston at the time.

One morning, about halfway through the summer, I sat down in my chair in the ministry office to begin my day. I had just had my first drink of coffee when the phone rang: it was Bonnie, a client, telling me that her husband had just killed their baby. I think I went into a kind of shock, unable to process the enormity of what had happened. I sleepwalked through the next few days, and within a couple of weeks I put the terrible events aside. Nine months later, I found myself writing that scene in the play—a scene so horrible that to this day I find it difficult to watch the play. In the first draft, the killing of the baby took place on the stage. In the subsequent editions, I revised the stage directions so that they instructed the actor to be OFFSTAGE when this happened, so that we can hear him talking but not see him with the baby. Somehow, after the fifth or sixth edition, this was lost—maybe because I am the most slipshod editor of my own work imaginable. Now, in this new edition, the killing is where it must be, offstage. When I became a mother it became clear to me that to see Alan strangle his baby would be unholy; nobody should see such a thing. We know that it happens, but to actually see it offends so deeply, so profoundly, that the viewer may never recover. It is enough to know that it happens, to hear that it has happened; the viewer can begin to absorb what has happened, and in the days following the performance perhaps ask themselves, how we, as the privileged class in our society, are implicated. How does this happen while we are in charge? How does this happen on our watch? This is the unimaginable happening, like the suicide of a young person. This scene must forever be offstage, and any director who goes against my wishes and puts the scene onstage, is, as far as I'm concerned, cursed. All this being said, I would never consider taking it out of the play because it is a true story, a tragedy that must be bellowed out to the world.

The first production of *The Crackwalker*, directed by the late Clarke Rogers, was in the beautiful back space at Theatre Passe Muraille. The rehearsals were fraught and very stressful, as Clarke, may he rest in peace, and I fought constantly, but I was generally thrilled with the actors—I loved how they were able to ride that line between humour and darkness so effectively. This play should have the audience laughing as much as crying, or it isn't working. The community was most generous and supportive in their response to the play, so much so that I was confident that the critics were going to give us raves.

I remember cycling in the pouring rain with my boyfriend Gregor Campbell, now my husband, to buy newspapers. I remember standing in the corner store and reading a dreadful pan of my first play. It was devastating. Only one critic, the late Gordon Vogt, also from Kingston, loved this play, and understood it. I survived this battering because to my great surprise Maurice Podbrey, the artistic director of Centaur Theatre decided to program it, at great risk, in his season. It was then that the great reviews began, and the Canadian community took notice. It really was a thrilling time, even watching as the audience left in droves, counted on an electronic clicker by an usher, saying things like "Call the chauffeur, George, we're leaving." Some of these audience members were landlords who owned the kind of slums that the characters in *The Crackwalker* live in, and they did not want to see the world that they had a part in creating.

Over the next thirty years, this play has been produced hundreds of times, in many languages, everywhere from New York to London to L.A. to Jerusalem to tiny little towns in faraway places. It has never been in a theatre larger than three hundred seats, and usually when it is produced it is in an even smaller theatre. To my great joy, it seems to be a favourite of young people, especially high-school and college or university students. I am glad to see that though it is very much set in the seventies, it seems to have transcended time. Occasionally I find myself irritated when somebody I am speaking to only knows about or cares about *The Crackwalker*. I imperiously remind them that I have written fourteen other plays, and each of them has been more important than life itself to me while I was writing it, while I was in rehearsal, and while I was watching, electrified, during the first run of each. But that all being said, there is nothing like the rush of your first-born baby, or your first-born play. I will always be grateful to the theatre goddess that granted me the gift of the play. Specifically, I am very grateful to the publisher, Playwrights Canada Press, who distributes this play so that people everywhere may read it, so that actors may perform it—and even more so, I am eternally grateful to the beautiful people who inspired this play, those deemed "permanently unemployable;" those who have been violently pushed to the margins of society; those who have not had a chance from the moment they were born; those who are either ignored or treated with contempt; those who will never travel out of the town they live in, unless it is to go to prison; those who will never swim in the ocean or climb a mountain or go to college or university or paint a picture or write a play, poem, or novel. They have been silenced by a well-meaning government and well-meaning citizens who are deeply uneasy, looking at and engaging with those whose very existence illuminates our insularity, our selfishness and greed, and worst of all, our abject fear of the Crackwalker in all of us.

—Judith Thompson
September, 2010

The Crackwalker was first produced by Theatre Passe Muraille, Toronto, in November, 1980, with the following company:

Theresa	JoAnn McIntyre
Sandy	Jane Foster
Alan	Hardee T. Lineham
Joe	Geza Kovacs
The Man	Graham Greene

Directed by Clarke Rogers
Set and costumes designed by Patsy Lang

Characters

Theresa
Sandy
Joe
Alan
The Man

Act One, Scene One

THERESA   Shut up, mouth, I not goin back there no more, no way, I'm goin back to Sandy's! *(to audience)* You know what she done to me? She make me go livin with her up on Division near Chung Wah's, 'cause she say I come from God, eh, then she go lookin in my room every night, see if I got guys in there 'cause Bonnie Cain told her I was suckin off queers down the Lido for five bucks; I wasn't doin it anyways, Bonnie Cain was doin it, I was just watchin. So last night, eh, I'm up there with a friend of mine, Danny, he a taxi driver — we're just talkin, eh, we weren't doin nothin, and so she come up and knock on the door and she say, "Trese, I know you got someone in there," and I go "No, Mrs. Beddison, ain't nobody in here," and she start goin on about God and that, and how she knowed 'cause she got a six feelin in her, so I get scared, eh, so I tell Danny to get in the closet. We don't got no clothes on, eh, so I put his jeans and that under the bed and I get under the covers like I'm sleepin and I go "S'kay, Mrs. Beddison, you could come in now." So she come in lookin at me like a stupid bitch and she say she knowed there was somebody in there 'cause she heard talkin and I says, "You feelin okay, Mrs. Beddison, ain't nobody here cept me and I sleepin," then she start goin near the closet, eh, and Danny start laughin. Well she run up the closet and she pullin on the door and I'm pullin on her arm and I'm saying, "Trust me, Mrs. Beddison, ya gotta trus me," 'cause the sosha workers are always goin on about trus and that, eh, but she don't listen, she open the door and there's Danny standin stripped naked. Well that whoredog Beddison start screamin God words at him, eh, so he takes off outta the house and she takes off after him, and I got his pants, eh, so I throw em out the window case he catch em, and then I bawlin. I bawlin on the bed and ya know what she make me do? She make me take a bath! A bubble bath like for the baby! All bubbles and that! Then she make me put on her stupid dressin robe, itch my skin and smell like chocolate bars and that, and she take me to where she livin and you know what she make me do? She make me read the Bible! I don't like readin no stupid Bible! Ya get a stomach ache doin that, ya do! Stupid hosebag. I'm not goin back there no more, no way, I'm goin back to Sandy's.

Act One, Scene Two

> SANDY and JOE's apartment. SANDY is scrubbing the floor furiously. THERESA appears, joyous, carrying a plastic bag containing all of her belongings. As she has not seen SANDY in several weeks, she is very excited.

THERESA   Hi, Sandy, how ya doin?

                SANDY does not look at THERESA.

SANDY   What are you doin here?

THERESA   I come callin on ya!

                *In the following sequence, SANDY's anger
                builds. At first, however, it contains an ele-
                ment of teasing.*

SANDY   I don't want no houndogs callin on me. *(contin-
                ues scrubbing)*

THERESA   I not a houndog!

SANDY   Yes, y'are.

THERESA   No I not.

SANDY   Whoredog houndog, that's what you are.

THERESA   *(laughs, delighted)* Sanny!

SANDY   *(pointing backwards)* And get your whorepaws
                offa my sofa.

THERESA   *(jumps, removes hand, gasps)* Sanny, like I don't
                mean to bug ya or nothin *(eating doughnut from
                bag)* but like I don't get off on livin where I'm
                livin no more so I come back here sleepin on the
                couch, okay?

SANDY   I not keepin no cow-pies here.

THERESA   I not a cow-pie!

SANDY   *(faces her)* Would you get out of my house?

THERESA   Why, what I done?

SANDY   …Ya smell like cookin fat—turns my gut.

THERESA   That only 'cause I eatin chip from the chip wagon!

SANDY   I don't care what it's 'cause of, get your whore-face out of here.

THERESA   Why, why you bein ugly for?

SANDY   You tell me and then we'll both know.

THERESA   What?

SANDY   Don't think nobody seen ya neither 'cause Bonnie Cain seen ya, right through the picture window!

             THERESA claps a hand to her mouth in "uh-oh."

             On my couch that I paid for with my money.

THERESA   Wha—

SANDY   With my husband!

THERESA	No way, Sanny.
SANDY	*(unable to contain her anger any longer)* You touch my fuckin husband again and I break every bone in your body!
THERESA	Bonnie Cain lyin, she lyin to ya, she think I took twenty buck off her, she tryin to get me back.
SANDY	*(starts speaking after "she lying to ya")* That's bullshit, Therese, 'cause Bonnie Cain don't lie and you know she don't.
THERESA	You don't trus me.
SANDY	Fuckin right.
THERESA	I never done it.
SANDY	Pretty bad combination, Trese, a retarded whore.
THERESA	That's a load of bullshit, Sanny, I *not retarded*.
SANDY	Just get out of my house and don't come back. *(pushes her)*
THERESA	No I never, I never done it! *(in angry indignation she pushes back)*
SANDY	Trese, Joe told me, he told me what the two of youse done!
THERESA	Oh.

SANDY   Lyin whore, look at ya, make me sick. Wearin
               that ugly dress, thinkin it's sexy 'cause it shows off
               your fat tits and those shoes are fuckin stupid, ya
               can't even walk in them.

THERESA   I know.

               SANDY *stares at* THERESA. THERESA *does not
               move.*

SANDY   *(with an air of resignation, tiredness)* Just get out,
               okay?

THERESA   I never wanted it, Sanny, I never wanted it, he
               come in, he made me.

SANDY   Bull, Trese.

THERESA   He did, I sleepin, I sleepin there havin dreams, I
               seen this puppy, and he come in and tie me up
               and push it in me down my hole.

SANDY   What?

THERESA   He tie me all up with strings and that and he sin-
               gin "Ol Macdonel Farm" and he say he gonna
               kill me if I don't shut up so I be quiet and he
               done it, he screw me.

SANDY   Are you shittin me?

THERESA   And—and—and he singin and he take his jean
               down and it all hard and smellin like pee pee
               and he go and he put it in my mouth.

SANDY	He could do twenty for that.
THERESA	Don't send him up the river, Sanny, he didn't mean nothin.
SANDY	Horny bastard, he's not gettin into me again.
THERESA	Me neither, Sanny, he tries anything I just run up to Tim Hortons, get a fancy doughnut.
SANDY	Oh he won't be cheatin on me again.
THERESA	How come, Sanny, you tell him off?
SANDY	Fuckin right I did. After Bonnie tole me, I start givin him shit, eh, and he takes the hand to me, callin me a hag and sayin how he liked pokin you bettern that and look. *(reveals bruise)*
THERESA	Bassard.
SANDY	He's done it before, but he won't do it again.
THERESA	Why, Sanny, you call the cops on him?
SANDY	*Right*.
THERESA	Did ya—
SANDY	Ya know my high heels? The shiny black ones I got up in Toronto?
THERESA	Yeah, they're sharp.

SANDY   *(obviously enjoying telling the story)* And he
             knows it, too. After he beat up on me he takes off
             drinkin, comes back about three just shit-faced,
             eh, and passes out cold? Well I'm there lookin at
             him snorin like a pig and I says to myself, "I'm
             gonna get this bastard," I'm thinkin of how when
             I seen my heels sittin over in the corner and then
             I know what I'm gonna do. So I take one of the
             heels and go over real quiet to where he's lyin,
             and ya know what I do? I take the heel and I rip
             the holy shit out of his back with it.

THERESA   JEEZ DID HE WAKE UP?

SANDY   Fuckin right he did. You shoulda seen him, first
             I guess he thought he was dreamin, eh, so he just
             lies there makin these ugly noises, burpin and
             that? And then he opens his eyes, and puts his
             hands up like a baby, eh, and then I seen him see
             the heel. Well I take off right out the back door
             and he's comin after me fit to kill, his eyes is all
             red, he's hissin, I am scared shitless; well he gets
             ahold of me and I says to myself, "Sandy, this is
             it. This is how you're gonna die. You got the bas-
             tard back and now you're gonna die for it." Well
             he is just about to send me to the fuckin angels
             when he stops; just like that and turns around
             and goes on to bed.

THERESA   How come he done that, Sanny?

SANDY   I didn't know at first either, then I figured it out.
             Cuttin him with the heel was the smartest thing
             I done. Ya see, he wasn't gonna kill me 'cause

he don't want to do time, eh, and he knew if he just beat up on me he'd never get no more sleep 'cause I'd do it again. He knows it. He don't dare take a hand to me again, no way. Either he takes off, or he stays and he treats me nice.

THERESA   Did you talk to him later?

SANDY   I ain't seen him for three days. But we ate to-gether before he took off, I fixed him up some tuna casserole and we ate it; we didn't say noth-in, though. It don't matter, we sometimes go a whole week without talkin, don't mean we're pissed off at each other.

THERESA   Al and I talkin all the time when we go out.

SANDY   We did too when we first started goin together. After a while ya don't have to talk 'cause you always know what they're gonna say anyways. Makes ya sick sometimes. What are you bawlin for?

THERESA   I'm sorry Joe done that to me, Sanny.

SANDY   He's like that, he's a prick.

THERESA   S'okay if I come livin here then?

SANDY   ...Sure, I don't care.

THERESA   Thank you, Sanny.

SANDY   I like the company.

THERESA   Don't say nothin to Al, eh?

SANDY   What if I tell him what Bonnie Cain tole me
           about you blowin off queers down the Lido?

THERESA   Oh no, Sanny, don't say bout that.

SANDY   I guess old fags in Kingston are pretty hard up.

THERESA   You want a doughnut, Sanny?

SANDY   No. What kind ya got?

THERESA   Apple fritters.

SANDY   Jeez, Therese, ya ever see how they make them
           things?

THERESA   No, I never worked up there.

SANDY   It'd make ya sick.

THERESA   I love em.

SANDY   I know ya do, you're a pig.

THERESA   Fuck off… Only kiddin.

SANDY   You watch your mouth.

THERESA   You love Joe still?

SANDY   I don't know. I used to feel like we was in the
           fuckin movies. Member that show *Funny Girl*

where Barbra Streisand and Omar Sharif are goin together?

THERESA   She hardly sing pretty.

SANDY   Well remember that part where they start singin right on the boat, singin to each other?

THERESA   Yeah.

SANDY   We done that once. We'd been up at the Manor, eh, Chesty Morgan was up there so we'd just been havin a hoot, eh, and Joe wants to go over to the General Wolfe to see the Mayor, so we get on the Wolfe Island ferry and we're laughin and carryin on and that and then we start singin, right on the bow of the Wolfe Island ferry.

THERESA   Jeez.

SANDY   We didn't care when we were doin it though, we didn't give a shit what anyone was thinkin, fuck em, we were havin fun.

THERESA   I love singin.

SANDY   Joe really done that to you?

THERESA   What?

SANDY   *Raped* ya.

THERESA   Don't like talkin about it, Sanny.

SANDY	*Trese.*
THERESA	He done it when I never wanted it, it's true.
SANDY	It is, eh?
THERESA	S'true, Sanny. Don't tell Joe, eh?
SANDY	I mighta known it.
THERESA	Still okay if I sleepin here though?
SANDY	You're gonna have to do the housework while I'm workin for Nikos.
THERESA	How come you workin down there, I thought you didn't like Nikos?
SANDY	I get off on corn beef on rye, arsewipe, what d'ya think, I need the fuckin money.
THERESA	Ain't Joe drivin for Amey's no more?
SANDY	No.
THERESA	What's he doin?
SANDY	Fuckin the dog, I don't know.
THERESA	Bassard.
SANDY	I know. Gimme a bite of that.
THERESA	I not really retarded, am I, Sanny?

SANDY	Just a little slow.
THERESA	Not like that guy walkin down street lookin at the sidewalk?
SANDY	Jeez he give me the creeps.
THERESA	He hardly got the long beard, eh?
SANDY	I know.
THERESA	Not like him, eh, Sanny?
SANDY	No. No, I tole ya, Therese, you're just a little slow.
THERESA	Oh.

> JOE *and* ALAN *barge in with a stolen motorbike. They start quickly, efficiently taking it apart and packing the parts.* SANDY *and* THERESA *stand there stupefied.*

JOE	Ya hoo! We got ourselves a shit-hot mother!
ALAN	Did we *ever*!
JOE	Okay nice and easy, we don't want to mark this babe.
ALAN	Like this?
JOE	That's right, buddy—fuckin back door wide open, shit that dog just sittin there waggin its tail at us.

ALAN   He wanted to be buddies with us.

JOE   I just about shit, it was fuckin helpin us.

THERESA   What kinda dog was it, Al, one of them golden?

JOE   A shepherd.

ALAN   A German shepherd, a police dog.

JOE   A fuckin screw dog.

SANDY   You're not bringin Martin over here.

JOE   How's my pussycake doin? Eh? (*kisses* SANDY) Eh
            pussycake?

SANDY   I says you're not bringin Martin over here.

JOE   Don't worry, babe, we're meetin him over to the
            Shamrock he ain't comin here.

ALAN   Down the Beachcomber Room.

THERESA   That's hardly nice down there, all them trees and
            that?

ALAN   You like it there?

THERESA   I love it.

ALAN   I'll take ya there sometime.

SANDY   Where you been the last three nights?

JOE	Paintin the town brown, honeysuck, whata you been doin?
SANDY	I said where were ya for three nights in a row?
JOE	Out with the Mayor, poochie, spookin out the Royal.
THERESA	You not out with him, he dead.
ALAN	Theresa.
THERESA	He is dead.
ALAN	Joe's only kiddin, Trese.
SANDY	You tell me where ya been or you're out on your ear. I said where were ya the last three nights?
JOE	Just hold on to your pants, sugar crack, first things first. *(madly working on the bike)*
ALAN	This is big bucks ya know.
SANDY	You don't have to tell me 'cause I know. I know where ya were, you were down the Embassy pissin our money away.
THERESA	Them ugly old Greeks down there anyways.
ALAN	You were takin Papa's *shirt*, eh Joe?
SANDY	I'll tell ya somethin about gamblers, youse do it just so's you could lose, it's true that's why.

JOE	Well fuck me blind I never knew that. Did you know that, Al?
ALAN	Nope, I never heard of that.
JOE	Thars pretty good commander, where'd ya get that offa?
SANDY	It happened to be in the *Reader's Digest*, arsewipe, and it was written by a doctor, Doctor John Grant, and I guess he knows what he's talkin about.
JOE	Oooooh *Reader's Digest*, shit-for-brains is going smart on us.
THERESA	She not a shit-for-brains you stupid.
JOE	You simmer down there, burger.
SANDY	Is that where ya were, pissin away my money?
JOE	*(completes a physical action)* Gotcha.
SANDY	Eh?
JOE	Hand me the pliers, would ya?
SANDY	*(screeching)* I said where were ya, Joe!

> JOE *spits his mouthful of beer in her face.*
> ALAN *laughs and laughs.*

That's cute.

THERESA   Stupid dummy-face.

            JOE spits on ALAN. ALAN laughs, spits back.

SANDY   You are cut off and I mean it.

JOE   From what, bitch, your ugly box?

            SANDY exits to clean up.

            Don't know what she's so pissed off at, nice brew
            in the face cool ya right down.

THERESA   I'm movin back here, Joe, Sanny said I could.

ALAN   She did?

JOE   Is that right.

THERESA   Sleepin on the couch, that okay, Joe?

JOE   Sure, fuck, I don't care, long as the two of youse
            don't gang up on me.

ALAN   Two women together always do.

THERESA   What do two women do?

ALAN   You know, gang up on the guy.

SANDY   *(entering)* Only if he got it comin to him.

JOE   Do I get it comin to me, commander?

SANDY   You're fuckin right you do.

JOE   Little diesel dyke this one, see what she done to me?

ALAN   Holy Jeez!

JOE   She's a live one all right, Pearl Lasalle the second.

THERESA   She not like Pearl Lasalle, Pearl Lasalle ugly lookin.

JOE   She fights like her though, don't ya honey suck? What's for supper I'm starvin.

SANDY   Nothin.

JOE   What?

SANDY   You don't bring in money, we don't get no supper.

JOE   Well fuck—don't we got stuff for samiches?

SANDY   Nope.

JOE   Well fuck, I'm goin over to Shirley's.

SANDY   When?

JOE   Right now fuck.

SANDY   Take your stuff with ya.

JOE   Would ya sit on this first, I want fish for supper.

SANDY   Pig. I says take your stuff with ya and get out.

JOE   You for real?

SANDY   Fuckin right.

JOE   All right I been wantin out of this hole. Thanks, babe.

SANDY   Is that right?

JOE   Take care. *(starts to go)*

SANDY   You could get in a lot of trouble rapin a retard, Joe.

JOE   Pardon?

SANDY   I said you could get in a lot of trouble rapin a retard.

                    THERESA is motioning "No! No! No!" to SANDY.

JOE   Yeah that's right you would. So?

SANDY   You'll be up the river for twenty years when I tell the cops what you done, Joe.

ALAN   Over fifty don't get you twenty years no way no way!

SANDY	I'm not talkin bout the bike.
JOE	What? What are ya talkin about eh?
SANDY	About rapin a retard.
JOE	What?
SANDY	About rapin Theresa.
JOE	What?
SANDY	About rapin Theresa with me in the next room.
JOE	Rape? Rape? Who told you that, did Theresa tell you that?
SANDY	Yeahhh.
THERESA	No no, Sanny, not rape, I only said he done it when I never wanted it.
JOE	Did you tell my wife that I raped you, Theresa? *(THERESA doesn't answer.)* Did you say that? Eh? *(grabs her)* Eh?
THERESA	I never—leave me alone, you big ugly cock—
JOE	I'll tell you somethin about your little girfriend buddy. I'll tell you something about this little—
ALAN	It don't matter, Joe, it—it—it just don't matter, nobody don't believe her anyways.

JOE   This little girl who's callin rape was sittin on that
             couch beggin for it.

ALAN   She never.

SANDY   Theresa?

JOE   It's true. I come in piss drunk, I'm passed out on
             the floor, and there she is down on all fours sh-
             ovin her big white ass in my face.

THERESA   No I never.

JOE   Big white bootie right in the face.

THERESA   Go away.

JOE   Tell em like it was Trese, and no crossin
             fingers.

THERESA   I never say that, Sanny, I never mean he rape
             me!

SANDY   Theresa, is he tellin the truth?

ALAN   Theresa, you never done that, did ya? Shown
             him your bum?

JOE   This is your last chance, burger, now tell the
             fuckin truth or I get serious.

SANDY   Don't lie to me Theresa. I can forgive a lot of
             things but not a lie.

ALAN   You can tell the truth, Theresa, I'll take care of
            ya.

SANDY   Eh, Trese?

            Pause.

THERESA   *(laughing)* Who farted?

ALAN   I never did.

JOE   Eh Theresa?

ALAN   It's—it's okay, Joe it's—she—she can't handle
            her booze yet, she was probably drunk or snif-
            fin and you was drunk and it don't matter, it just
            don't matter, I'll be stayin with her all the nights
            from now, I'm gonna take care of her it won't
            happen again, she won't never say nothin bout
            ya again I promise.

THERESA   You stayin with me all nights from now, Al?

ALAN   I'm takin care of ya. I'm—

SANDY   Could youse leave us alone, please.

ALAN   Who, me and Theresa?

SANDY   If you don't mind.

ALAN   Sure, sure. We—

THERESA	Wait for me, Al, I wanna get some chocolate bars and that, I starvin… well I am, I didn't have no dinner.
JOE	You. You watch your mouth, eh?
SANDY	Would youse just take off?

ALAN pulls THERESA out.

| THERESA | See youse later, don't do nothin I wouldn't do. |

Act One, Scene Three

ALAN and THERESA exit. JOE is furious and trying to cool down. His back is to SANDY. She is aware of his anger. She picks something up off the kitchen floor and starts to take it into the kitchen. JOE grabs her as she tries to pass him and throws her to the floor.

JOE	You CUNT.
SANDY	Keep away from me —
JOE	I'm a fuckin rapist 'cause a fuckin retard SAYS so?
SANDY	Touch me again and you go to your goddamn grave!

JOE	FUCK maybe I'm the maniac been carvin all the TELLERS out in SASKATOON! *(makes monster face and noise)*
SANDY	Go jump in a hole.
JOE	*(grabs her, hard)* What is fuckin with your BRAIN, woman?
SANDY	I didn't mean it.
JOE	It was a *joke*?
SANDY	I was just—you said you liked her better.
JOE	What?
SANDY	You said you liked—pokin her better.
JOE	*(laughs, almost hysterically)* So I go to the joint.
SANDY	I wasnt gonna tell nobody—
JOE	You're a fuckin CROW, you know that?
SANDY	I was just—seein—
JOE	*(thrusting her away)* Get away from me.

> SANDY *starts to run toward him, trying to scream but the sound is muffled and distorted by a stomach seizure, that stopping her about three feet away from* JOE.

You got your upset stomach again?

SANDY Bastard.

JOE *(looks her up and down)* You just give me a hard-on.

> SANDY *spits on him.*

Hewww, you like it when I'm rough with ya, don't ya? Eh? *(moves her roughly, whispers)* Makes your nips stand up when I'm rough with ya.

> SANDY's *hands are still raised.* SANDY *and* JOE *are a foot apart throughout the exchange.* SANDY *looks at him with hatred.*

What, you don't want it? Okay, see ya later!

> *He starts to leave.*

SANDY *(head down)* Joe.

JOE What can I do for ya?

> SANDY *smiles.*

Oh, ya do want it. Okay, why—why—don't ya take that blouse there off?

> *She removes her blouse.*

Hm. And the skirt.

She removes her skirt. She is left in a bra and pantyhose with a low crotch. He nods, looking her up and down.

How come ya like it like this? Eh? *(shakes his head)* I gotta be somewhere.

JOE exits. SANDY remains on stage, not moving. Lights out quickly.

Act One, Scene Four

THERESA and ALAN are in a restaurant.

THERESA   Where d'ya think Joe took off to?

ALAN   I don't know probably drinkin, maybe the Shamrock.

THERESA   You think they're splitting up?

ALAN   I hope not.

THERESA   Me too. I love Sandy, she my best girlfriend.

ALAN   I—Joe—he and me are good buddies, too. They go good together anyways.

THERESA   Could I have a doughnut?

ALAN   What kind, chocolate? I know you like chocolate.

THERESA   I love it.

ALAN   Sandy's nuts, you're not fat.

THERESA   Don't say nothin about it.

ALAN   You're not.

THERESA   I don't like talkin about it.

ALAN   Here. Two chocolate donuts.

THERESA   Thank you, Alan.

ALAN   Jesus you're a good-lookin girl. You're the pretti-
            est lookin girl I seen.

THERESA   Don't talk like that.

ALAN   I love screwin with ya. Do you like it with me?

THERESA   I don't know—don't ask me that stuff, dummy-face.

ALAN   I like eatin ya out ya know.

THERESA   Shut your mouth, people are lookin, don't talk
            like that, stupid-face.

ALAN   Nobody's lookin. Jeez you're pretty. Just like a lit-
            tle angel. Huh. Like a—I know. I know. I'm gon-
            na call you my little angel from now on. People
            gonna see ya and they're gonna go "There's
            Trese, she's Al's angel!"

THERESA   Who gonna say them things?

ALAN   Anybody.

THERESA   They are?

ALAN   Yup.

THERESA   You're a dummy-face.

ALAN   So beautiful.

THERESA   Stop it, Al, you make me embarrass.

ALAN   You're—I was always hopin for someone like
           you—always happy, always laughin and that.

THERESA   I cryin sometimes ya know.

ALAN   Yeah but ya cry the same way ya laugh. There's
           somethin—I don't know—as soon as I seen ya I
           knew I wanted ya. I wanted to marry ya when I
           seen ya.

THERESA   When, when did you say that?

ALAN   I never said nothin, I just thought it, all the
           time.

THERESA   We only been goin together for a little while, you
           know.

ALAN   Let's get married.

THERESA	Al, stop lookin at me like, that you embarrassin me.
ALAN	Sorry. Did you hear me?
THERESA	Yeah. Okay.
ALAN	When?
THERESA	Tuesday. I ask my sosha worker to come.
ALAN	No. Just Joe and me and you and Sandy. Just the four of us. I want Joe to be my best man.
THERESA	Sandy could be the flower girl. Uh. Oh.
ALAN	What?
THERESA	Hope you don't want no babies.
ALAN	Why? I do! I do want babies! I get on with babies good!
THERESA	Not sposda have none.
ALAN	How come? Who told you that?
THERESA	The sosha worker, she say I gotta get my tubes tied.
ALAN	What's that?
THERESA	Operation up the hospital. They tie it up down there so ya won't go havin babies.

ALAN   They can't do that to you no way!

THERESA   I know they can't but they're doin it.

ALAN   They don't have no right.

THERESA   Yah they do, Al, I slow.

ALAN   Slow? I don't think you're slow, who told YOU
            that?

THERESA   I ain't a good mum, Al, I cant help it.

ALAN   Who said you ain't a good mum?

THERESA   All of them just 'cause when I took off on Dawn.

ALAN   Who's Dawn?

THERESA   The baby, the other baby.

ALAN   You never had a baby before, did ya? Did ya?

THERESA   Las—

ALAN   You didn't have no other man's baby, did ya?
            With another guy?

            Pause.

THERESA   No, it's Bernice's.

ALAN   Who's Bernice?

THERESA   My cousin, my mum's sister.

ALAN   Well how come you were lookin after her baby?

THERESA   'Cause she was sick up in hospital. Jeez, Al.

ALAN   Well—what happened, whatdja do wrong?

THERESA   Nothin it wasn't my fault just one Friday night
          I was sniffin, eh, so I took off down to the plaza
          and I leave the baby up the room, eh, I thought
          I was comin right back, and I met this guy and
          he buyin me drinks and that, then I never knew
          what happened and I woke up and I asked some-
          body where I was and I was in Ottawa!

ALAN   He took you all the way up to Ottawa? That
          bastard.

THERESA   I never seen him again, I thumbed back to
          Kingston. *(crying)* I come back to the house and
          the baby's gone, she ain't there, so I bawlin. I
          goin everywhere yellin after her and never found
          nothin then I see Bonnie Cain and she told me
          they took her up the Children's Aid, she dead.
          So I go on up the Aid and they say she ain't dead
          she live but they not givin her back 'cause I unfit.

ALAN   Jeez.

THERESA   I ain't no more, Al, I don't sniff or nothin.

ALAN   Them bastards.

THERESA   Honest.

ALAN   I know. I know ya don't and we're gonna have a
           baby and nobody ain't gonna stop us. We're gon-
           na have our own little baby between you and me
           and nobody can't say nothin 'bout it. You're not
           goin to no hospital, understand?

THERESA   But, Al, she say she gonna cut off my pension
           cheque if I don't get my tubes tied.

ALAN   Fuck the pension cheque you're not goin to no
           hospital.

THERESA   Okay, Al.

ALAN   Come here. You're not goin to no hospital.

THERESA   You won't let em do nothin to me, will ya, Al?

ALAN   Nope. You're my angel and they ain't gonna
           touch you… Hey! I know what ya look like
           now!

THERESA   What, a angel?

ALAN   That—that Madonna lady; you know them pic-
           tures they got up in classrooms when you're a
           kid? Them pictures of the Madonna?

THERESA   The Virgin Mary?

ALAN   Yeah. Her.

THERESA   I love her, I askin her for stuff.

ALAN   Yuh look just like her. Just like the Madonna.
           'Cept the Madonna picture got a baby in it.

THERESA   It do?

ALAN   She's holdin it right in her arms. You too, maybe,
           eh? Eh? Hey! Let's go up to the Good Thief.

THERESA   Al, I don't know you goin to church! You goin
           every Sunday?

ALAN   No I never went since I was five I just want to
           go now. We'll go and we'll—we'll like have a
           party lightin candles and that, a party for gettin
           married!

THERESA   I love lightin candles.

ALAN   Maybe the Father's gonna be there. They're al-
           ways happy when someone's gettin married, we
           could tell him!

THERESA   Al, I gettin sleepy.

ALAN   Well after we party I'm gonna put ya right down
           to sleep over at Joe's. I won't try nothin or nothin.

THERESA   What if Sandy be piss off.

ALAN   No, Trese, they said we could stay there together.
           The two of us. And we're gonna.

THERESA   Okay… really I lookin like that Madonna?

ALAN   Just like her. Just like her.

He is rocking her in his arms. Lights fade.

Act One, Scene Five

JOE   Me and the Mayor we'd pick up a couple steak hoagies, and a case of twenty-four, head up to Merton on the hogs—catch some shit group— you know, Mad Dog Fagin, Grapes of Wrath, somethin, get shitfaced then go back to Kingston, pick us up some juicy pie down at Lino's or Horny Tim's, drive it out to Middle Road, fuck it blind, and have em home by one o'clock. Then we'd go down and catch the last ferry to the island and fuckin ride from one end to the other all fuckin night. Seven o'clock we'd go into Lou's, have us some home fries and a couple eggs over easy then head on back to work in Kingston. That was when I was drivin a Cat makin a shitload of money just a shitload. Huh—the Mayor was fuckin crazy, wasn't nothin he wouldn't do—nothin— he was smart too, he went to university in the States even, he just didn't give a shit about it, you know? He had about a hundred books, I seen em all filled with words that long *(measures two feet)*, he knew what they meant, too, every one of them but he never let on, ya know? He never let on he knew so much… we never *talked* about shit, it was the shit we done together made us good buddies. Just doin stuff with a guy you know you're thinkin the same. Anybody touched him I woulda killed them and same goes for him... he was a damn good driver too but he wasn't drivin, Martin was. Fuckin Martin fuckin stoned on STP. Martin—Martin wasn't an asshole, but he stupid, you know? Jeez he was stupid. So this Friday night we'd all gotten pissed up the Manor, eh, then we all went over to the island just to fuck around and to see the Mayor's sister, Linda, who was workin at the General Wolfe waitin on tables. So Bart, that was his real name, Bart and me and Martin had all got these new boots over at the A1 men's store, really nice you know, all leather, real solid, a hundred bucks a pair so we wanted to show em off to Linda, you know, bug her. So Bart gets in there and he's jumpin on tables, eatin all the limes and cherries and that for the drinks, singin some gross song about his love boots, he called them. Fuck it was funny— we were killin ourselves but Linda, she wasn't laughin, her boss was gettin pissed off so she told Bart, she goes, "Bart, get the fuck out of here I think your goddamn boots are shit." That's what she said. So he give her a big kiss right in front of her boss and we take off in Martin's car. Me and the Mayor in the back seat, Martin and his girlfriend in the front. Well we're headin down the road goin south, it's dark but it ain't wet and the last thing I remember Bart looks at me and he says, "I wonder what it's like to fuck an angel," and bang everything goes fuckin black. When I come to I'm in the fucking ambulance goin across to Kingston and Bart's lyin there beside me dead only I didn't know it and there's his sister Linda right there in the ambulance. I don't know how she got there—she's all red all black under her eyes and that and she's bawlin just bawlin up a storm and she's huggin his legs and she's sayin something only I can't make out what she's sayin, I can't make it out, I was so out of it I'm thinkin I'm gonna die I'm thinkin I'm gonna die if I don't make out what she's sayin so I kept tryin to make it out and she kept sayin it and then I knew what she was sayin and you know what it was? …She was sayin she did like his boots. "I do like your boots Bart I do like your boots Bart I do like your boots I do like your fuckin boots I do like your boots I do like your boots I do like your boots…" She wouldn't fuckin stop it.

Act One, Scene Six

> ALAN *and* THERESA *are sound asleep. The room is sometimes lit by passing cars. Noise of people on the street.* THERESA's *steady breathing. Suddenly we hear* JOE, *very drunk, half singing. As soon as* ALAN *hears him he springs into his jeans, legs shaking, and awkwardly tries to light a cigarette. His heart is racing.* JOE *enters.*

ALAN   Hey Joe.

JOE   Jeeeeeeezus you gimme a scare, what are you doin here?

ALAN   Stayin with Trese, member? Member ya said I
           could? The—the mum's got company—in from
           Windsor.

JOE   Windsor—What a fuckin hole.

ALAN   Yeah it's hot down there—in the summer—

JOE   Look what I found in the fuckin hallway. Cheese
           samich with a bloody kleenex stuck to it.

           This makes ALAN *very sick.*

ALAN   Jeezus, who put it there.

JOE   I was thinkin maybe the wife left out a little
           snack for me. Ya want some? Blood 'n Cheez
           Whiz samich? Hey hey hey it's hardly good.

ALAN   Hey no—no—no thank you. No way.

JOE   What, you don't like eatin blood or somethin?

ALAN   I never tried it.

JOE   Were you screwin that?

ALAN   No! No I mean no I was just I—

JOE   Why the hell not?

ALAN   Oh no I mean I was eh, like I was a couple hours
           ago, but not right before ya came in I wasn't.

JOE	Jeez you're strange. How come ya got dressed, you goin out?
ALAN	No—no I'm not goin out—I—I couldn't fuckin sleep, you know? Ya know what that's like? Ya just keep turnin and can't lie right? So I thought I'd wait up and just shoot the shit with you when ya came in.
JOE	Strange-o.
ALAN	I guess so. Didju play tonight?
JOE	Papadapa dies!
ALAN	He—he was cheatin again?
JOE	Fuckin right he was.
ALAN	He dies.
JOE	Greasy fuck. Fuck, once I seen Edwards get him in a half nelson an he was so greasy he slipped out!
ALAN	Ewwww.
JOE	Slipped right out. Slimy bastard, right in the middle of the game I turn to him and I says, "Papa," I says, "Don't fuck with me, just don't fuck with me."
ALAN	That's hardly good. Huh. What did he say?

JOE	Nothin. He just made one of them noises.
ALAN	What, what the ones with their mouth like this? Like a chicken does?
JOE	Hah. Yeah it is kinda like a chicken. Gives me the creeps.
ALAN	Yeah. Yeah, they do that all the time and the one I worked for, Andy? He *stunk* too, he smelled like matches, you know? After ya light a match?
JOE	He's gettin it.
ALAN	Yeah? Yeah? Who's gonna give it to him, are you? Are you gonna give it to him, Joe? I'll help ya, I hate the bastard. I hate him.
JOE	Buddy I am pleadin the Fifth. Fuuuck. *(singing)* "I gotta get outtaaa this place if it's the lassst…"
ALAN	I know what ya mean, Joe. Too—too—too bad there weren't no late movie on or something— hah—*Mr. Ed* or somethin.
JOE	Who's he when he's at home?
ALAN	Mr. Ed? The talkin horse, don't ya remember? "A horse is a horse of course of course and no one…"
JOE	Hey *(indicating bedroom)*, w'she bawlin or did she go out?

ALAN	Sleepin when we come in I think.
JOE	She's a good woman, buddy.
ALAN	I know she is, Joe. So's Trese.
JOE	Are you sure, buddy?
ALAN	Oh—that was—she—she didn't mean nothin, honest, Joe, she she just don't think sometimes, ya know?
JOE	That mouth of hers is gonna send her up shit creek one day, ain't it, burger?
ALAN	You—you want a smoke?
JOE	Whaddya got—menthol, fuck, I can't smoke that shit.
ALAN	I know—I didn't buy em, a guy a guy give em to me.
JOE	Hey, hamburger, sorry for wakin ya.
THERESA	I not a hamburger.
JOE	Ooooh I thought ya was!
THERESA	You shut up, I sleepin.
JOE	Okay, burger queen. Yeah. Yeah, buddy, she's okay too.

ALAN   Thank you, Joe. So's Sandy.

JOE   She never fucked around on me, you know.

ALAN   No?

JOE   Not once. *(goes to window and leans out)* What a fuckin hole this is, eh? ...K fuckin O. *(yells out window)* Fuuuuuuck.

            SANDY enters.

SANDY   Would you shut it?

JOE   *(singing)* "I gotta get out of this place."

SANDY   Why don't ya then, ya big pig.

JOE   I told ya, woman, don't go callin me pig in public. Jeez she got an ugly mouth, eh?

SANDY   You're shitfaced, Joe, go on and pass out.

JOE   You make me wanta piss my pants.

SANDY   Just go on makin a fool of yourself.

JOE   Down, woman, me and my pal Al is gonna head up to Horny Tim's and we're gonna pick us up some tailerooonie! Then we're gonna go on over to the quarry and we're gonna get ourselves sucked and fucked—

SANDY   You're not proud, are ya.

> JOE *bumps into something, falls.* SANDY *starts to pick him up.*

JOE   You never fooled around on me, did ya?

SANDY   Nope. I never… did.

JOE   *(sings)* "She's a hooo-o-o-o-nky tonk womannnn gimme *(goes to the bedroom)* gimme gimme the *(fading)* honky tonk wom…"

> ALAN *goes to the window and silently mouths "Fuuuuck," in imitation of* JOE. *He turns on the* TV, *crouches on the sofa, and sings softly, but can't remember the whole song.*

ALAN   Nobody—nobody here—but us chickens, nobody here but us guys don't—don't bother me we got work—to do we got stuff to do and eggs to lay—we're busy—chickens— *(He pretends to be a car, makes sounds, mimes a steering wheel.)* Neeowwwwwwwwwww. Whaaaaaa. Fhrhuuummmm. Atta girl.

Act One, Scene Seven

> *Later,* SANDY *brings in bedding to sleep on the sofa, turns on the lamp, turns off the* TV, *lights a cigarette, sits on the sofa.*

SANDY   He pukes all over the fuckin bed.

ALAN   Oooh shit.

SANDY   Funny.

ALAN   I'm—I'm sorry, Sandy, I didn't mean to laugh at ya.

SANDY   Can I ask you a personal question?

ALAN   Yeah, yeah sure—what?

SANDY   Am I gettin ugly lookin?

ALAN   What?

SANDY   You know, mean lookin, uglier lookin.

ALAN   Shit no, jeez—you—you look nice I think ya do! Who, who said that?

SANDY   No one. Are ya sure?

ALAN   Sure, sure I am, you're a good looker I even heard people say ya was.

SANDY   Who, who said that?

ALAN   Alf. Alf said ya was.

SANDY   His folks are loaded.

ALAN   I know!

SANDY   Did—did Joe ever say anything?

ALAN   Joe? What about?

SANDY   About me gettin ugly, *arsewipe*.

ALAN   No, no Joe never said nothin.

SANDY   Are ya sure?

ALAN   Yeah. Yeah he never—he never said nothin! No!
              Why?

SANDY   None of your business.

ALAN   What's buggin you, you got your pains?

SANDY   No, I don't got my pains but I'm gonna get em
              if youse—if youse—well—no offence or nothin
              but when are youse gettin outta here anyways?

ALAN   Soon as I get up the money I—wh—why is—is it
              buggin you me and Trese sleepin over?

SANDY   Yeah. Yeah, it is it's—it's me and Joe gotta have—
              have some privacy, ya know? Ya know?

ALAN   Yeah. Yeah I do I—I'll be out soon, what can I
              say, we'll be out as soon as I got the cash.

SANDY   I never heard of screwin your girlfriend on your
              buddy's floor.

ALAN   I'll be out as soon as I got the cash, okay?

SANDY   It's just strange you goin with Trese on our floor.

ALAN   I know it's strange I know I'm strange I'm strange, okay?

SANDY   I know you're fuckin strange all right.

ALAN   You're smokin too much. You're smokin too much.

SANDY   Look who's talkin.

ALAN   Well at least I know I'm doin it, you don't even know. *(takes drag off cigarette)*

SANDY   You're fuckin nuts, you know that, nuts.

ALAN   I may be nuts but I fuckin know what I'm doin. I know I'm killin myself smokin these, I know it so I'm throwin them away, okay? I'm throwin them away!

            ALAN rips up his cigarettes and takes SANDY's cigarette out of her mouth.

            Fuckin killsticks!

SANDY   *(tries to stop him)* Stop it, you—fuckin don't you touch me—you fucker, you give me back the cash for those right now, right now, hear?

ALAN   No! No, Sandy, I can't, I don't have the money, I gotta save it so I can fuck off outta this hole, I don't have money, okay?

SANDY   *(starts to back out the door shaking her head)* You're nuts, Al—

ALAN   *(grabs her back into the room)* I am not nuts. I am not nuts, you understand? I just decided now I'm gonna quit smoking that's all. I got a flash in my head of my old man tryin to take his breath, tryin to find the fuckin air and not gettin it fuckin all hunched over so's he wouldn't drown to death, his his his feet all puffed, all that shit all that shit comin out of his mouth and they wouldn't even clean it 'cause they said he couldn't get nothin 'cause he was gonna die so he had all this shit comin out of his mouth and and I know he didn't like it 'cause he was clean—all the time he was washin—and then when he's dyin they don't give a shit about his goddamn mouth with all the fuck comin out of it and they got a goddamn vacuum cleaner goin—we can't hear nothin and he keeps sort of movin forward, movin ahead in his chair like when you're tryin not to crash out at the show so ya keep movin forward? He didn't want to go he didn't want to go at all and he went 'cause of these. 'Cause of these goddamn ugly white killsticks these! *(shows her cigarette, lets her go)* See? See why ya can't smoke? See?

SANDY   *(very moved by ALAN's speech; speaks quietly)* I don't know who the fuck you think you are tearin up the place just 'cause you seen your old man fuckin croak.

ALAN   You don't know what it's like, man, you don't know what it's like till you been there, dont you talk.

SANDY   Don't tell me what I know, arsewipe, don't you tell me nothin. I seen my mum go, I sat by her bed for three fuckin months and I don't go carryin on like a three-year-old.

ALAN   It wasn't the same, I'm tellin ya it couldna been the same.

SANDY   And I'm a woman and I don't go cryin about it, I never cried about it once.

ALAN   I'm not cryin about it, I never cried about it, I'm just tellin ya why not to smoke.

SANDY   You're just tellin me shit. Jeez if Joe seen you just now he'd think you were some kind of fag.

ALAN   I'm not a fag, that's one thing I'm not, I'm not a fag.

SANDY   Then start acting like a fuckin man.

ALAN   I'm not a fag, you take that back.

SANDY   I'm not takin nothin back for no baby.

ALAN   I said take that back, you ugly bitch.

        ALAN *grabs her.* SANDY *throws him to the floor.*

SANDY   You're sad, you know that? You don't scare nobody.

ALAN   I'm no fag.

SANDY   *(goes back to lie on the couch)* I seen ten-year-
          olds fight better than you.

ALAN   Why?

SANDY   Why what?

ALAN   Why don't I scare nobody?

SANDY   'Cause you're a wimp, that's why. Like one of
          them dogs that starts shakin when ya go to pat
          it.

ALAN   How come.

SANDY   How am I supposed to know?

ALAN   Don't say nothin to Joe, eh?

SANDY   What, about takin a fit?

ALAN   About you thinkin I'm like one of them dogs.

SANDY   I won't.

ALAN   Or Trese.

SANDY   Don't worry about it.

ALAN   You watched your mum go?

SANDY   Big deal.

ALAN   Couldna been the same.

SANDY	It's all the same.
ALAN	Don't you feel nothin?
SANDY	Well I'm not a baby like you.
ALAN	No.
SANDY	Anyways, bein dead ain't no different from livin anyways.
ALAN	How do you know?
SANDY	I just know. It's just like movin to Brockville or Oshawa or somethin. It ain't that different.
ALAN	Oh no. Oh no you're wrong, I think you're wrong there.
SANDY	No I'm not.
ALAN	Yes you are.
SANDY	You don't know shit, Al.
ALAN	I do, I do know some things and I know that. I know it's different.
SANDY	Get out of my house.
ALAN	I'm goin, I didn't want to stay anyways, it smells funny in here.
SANDY	Garbage stinks up a place.

ALAN   And Sandy.

SANDY   *What?*

ALAN   No offence or nothin, but you—you—are—you
            are gettin ugly lookin.

            SANDY looks at him.

            See ya.

Act One, Scene Eight

            *JOE, SANDY, ALAN, THERESA sitting in a bar.
            Otis Redding's "I've Been Loving You Too
            Long" is playing.*

JOE   That's a shit-hot tune. Too bad he died.

ALAN   Did he die?

JOE   Thats right. In a fuckin motel.

ALAN   That's too bad.

JOE   Too bad Jimi Hendrix died too.

ALAN   Yeah. Oh *yeah*. *(sings, drums)* "Scuse me while I
            kiss the sky!"

JOE   Did youse know if Hendrix hadda lived he was
            gonna join up with E.L.P.?

SANDY	I seen them, Emerson, Lake and Palmer, down in Montreal.
JOE	Ya know what they woulda been called if Hendrix hadda joined up with them?
ALAN	Hendrix, and…
JOE	*(wits it out)* H.E.L.P. Help. And you fuckin would need help hearin those two play together.
ALAN	Fuck would ya ever.
JOE	Fuckin straight.
ALAN	Would ya ever. Fuck, your brain'd die.
JOE	H.E.L.P. *Help.*
THERESA	I wouldn't need no help.
SANDY	You don't got no ear for music.
THERESA	I do so.
ALAN	She sings and that all the time.
THERESA	I seen Jerry uptown, he got a job workin for Wilmot's.
SANDY	That right, eh.
JOE	Splinter, what a cocksuck.

> *Restless,* JOE *goes to the jukebox, presses a button.* JOE *walks to the bathroom. After a moment* ALAN *follows.*

THERESA   He be workin with all that ice cream all the time.

> *Pause.*

SANDY   He could hardly munch out.

THERESA   I love ice cream.

SANDY   Just munch right out.

Act One, Scene Nine

> JOE *and* ALAN. *In the bathroom of the bar.*

ALAN   Those two guys together. Geez! *(shaking head in disbelief)*

JOE   I'm goin, buddy, I'm takin off.

ALAN   Where ya goin?

JOE   That's for me to know.

ALAN   Oh. Sorry. How—how come, gettin sick of Kingston?

JOE   Got me a job drivin a Cat.

ALAN	Jeez. You make a lot of cash doin that.
JOE	Nice work if you can get it.
ALAN	Nice work if you can get it.
JOE	Make a shitload of money.
ALAN	That's hard to do, drivin one of them things, ain't it?
JOE	They're motherfuckers.
ALAN	Jeez fuck, where'd ya learn how to do that anyways?
JOE	Hymie Beach.
ALAN	wow, I never knew that. You live down there?
JOE	Sure, shared a motel room with this creep who later turned out to be a queer boy. Started sayin stuff about my dink and that when I got out of the shower. "Is it always that long?"
ALAN	Fuckin queers.
JOE	I know.
ALAN	They just make me—feel like pukin—
JOE	I sent that one through the fuckin wall.
ALAN	Did ya?

JOE   Fuckin right.

ALAN   I hate em.

             Pause.

JOE   Don't say nothin to Sandy.

ALAN   Don't she know?

             JOE shakes his head.

             What if something happens—she gets cancer or
             somethin?

JOE   What?

ALAN   Them things happen, I've heard of them.

JOE   …I'll let ya know where I am.

ALAN   Hey—I'd like to do that kind of shit.

JOE   You should come out. You could get on a site
             drywallin or somethin.

ALAN   They just take anybody?

JOE   Sure.

ALAN   No, no way.

JOE   Suit yourself.

ALAN	Hey—I forgot to tell ya, Cathy Yachuk jumped offa the Brock Towers!
JOE	What?
ALAN	Jumped right onto her feet Martin was sayin, fucked em up so bad they hadda take a piece of her bum and glue it on to her f-f-feet—so's she could walk on them.
JOE	How come she done that?
ALAN	She seen a white light in front of her, tellin her!
JOE	Fuckin whore… yuh, I'm gettin right out of this hole.
ALAN	You comin back ever?
JOE	How'm I sposda know?

Act One, Scene Ten

ALAN on his way to work, stumbles out the door. There is a First Nations MAN on the street, his wrists bleeding heavily. He is ambling past ALAN. He is very drunk.

ALAN	Hey buddy—hey can I do something for ya?
MAN	*(drunk, mumbling)* Please…

ALAN	Hey, want a smoke?

| MAN | Yeah. Give me a smoke. |

| ALAN | What are ya lookin for, man? |

| MAN | Fuckers took it fuckers. |

| ALAN | Who? Did somebody jump ya? Eh? Did somebody jump ya? |

| MAN | Yaah. Some guys. Buncha Indians—fuckin Indians. |

| ALAN | Hey, man, you're an Indian aren't ya? |

| MAN | *(giggling)* Don't burn the fishbones! Don't burn the fishbones! |

| ALAN | That's okay, man, my fiancée, she's Indian. Therese. I like Indians it's okay. |

| MAN | *(weeping like a girl)* Stupid fuckin Indians. |

| ALAN | Hey. Hey don't cry. Is it hurtin bad? Please—just stay here—I'll call an ambulance. Stay. *(starts to walk to phone, holds up hand)* Stay. |

| MAN | *(sits up, screams a death scream)* Aaaahh! |

> ALAN *comes back, takes off his own shirt, ties it around the* MAN'S *wrist to stop the bleeding. The* MAN *sees a vision.*

Devil-baby-eyes-devil-baby-eyes. Please. Please.
Mercy. Mercy. Hand. Gimme your hand. Hand.
Please.

ALAN   What? You want me to hold your hand? Okay.

> MAN *takes* ALAN'S *hand, starts rubbing it in a*
> *sexual way.* ALAN *doesn't know what to do.*

MAN   *(urgently)* Hey. Hey. Hey.

ALAN   What, what is it, buddy?

MAN   Hey. *(makes intercourse motion with fingers)* Let's
tear off a piece. Come on, let's tear off a piece.
Rip off a piece. Come on.

ALAN   Stupid cocksucker!

> ALAN *flings* MAN *away, but* MAN *clings to his*
> *leg.*

Get off me, you fucker! Get offffffffff me! *(He*
runs.)

MAN   *(lies on street, giggling)* Pleeeease. (giggles)

> ALAN *jumps back to* SANDY'S *living room where*
> THERESA *is asleep at his feet.*

ALAN   *(yells)* Dieeeeeeeeeeee!

Act One, Scene Eleven

It is the middle of the night.

ALAN   Therese?

THERESA   Yeah?

ALAN   Do you ever start thinkin ugly thoughts before ya
            go to sleep?

THERESA   No, do you?

ALAN   Yeah.

THERESA   Like what?

ALAN   Like fallin down and your teeth hittin the
            sidewalk.

THERESA   Ewwwww.

ALAN   Sometimes I even think of someone takin out
            my spine, like they do with a shrimp.

THERESA   You crazy stupid-face, go sleepin and think of
            nice stuff.

ALAN   Like what?

THERESA   Doughnuts and the Wolfe Island ferry and that.
            Stuff like that.

ALAN   Huh. I love ya, Trese.

THERESA   Madonna.

Act Two, Scene One

ALAN   Did you ever start thinkin somethin, and it's like ugly…? And ya can't beat it out of your head? I wouldn't be scared of it if it was sittin in front of me, I'd beat it to shit—nothin wouldn't stop me—but I can't beat it 'cause it's in my head, fuck. It's not like bein crazy, it's just like thinkin one thing over and over and it kinda makes ya sick. Like when I was a kid and I used to have these earaches all the time, you know? And I would keep thinkin it was like a couple of garter snakes with big ugly teeth all yellow, like an old guy's teeth, and there they were the two of them suckin and bitin on my eardrum with these yellow teeth. Makin noises like a cat eatin cat food. I could even hear the fuckin noises. *(makes the noise)* Like that. Just made me wanta puke thinkin that—made the pain worse. I'd think of their eyes, too, that made me sick, black eyes lookin sideways all the time while they keep suckin and chewin on my eardrum. Fuck. Do youse know what I mean? No offense or nothin, I don't mean no offense, I wish youse all good luck in your lives. I was just—like I just wanted to know if any of youse like knew of a medicine or somethin ya might take for this—they gotta have somethin 'cause the one I'm thinkin of now is even worse, it's fuckin bad, it's it's somethin Bonnie Cain told me about this nurse she knows goin out to Enterprise, out to one of the farms out there, these folks were on the dole so she goes up to see if the kids got colds and that, and the wife, all small with her teeth all black takes her into the warshroom and tells her she got somethin wrong down in her woman's part. And Bonnie said this nurse lifted up this woman's skirt and you know what she seen? Like a cauliflower growin out of her thing! A cauliflower! Fuck! And ya know the worst part of it? When ya cut it it bleeds! It grows blood and that! It just happened last summer too, last fuckin summer in July! ...How'd she go—like how'd she pee? Fuck I'll be doin the dishes where I'm workin down the Tropicana there and it's like pictures burning holes in my brain, I try all the time to like put other pictures overtop of that, nice things that I really get off on, eh, that I really like like— like lambs in a field, you know, with the black on their faces? Like baby sheep? I always liked them, whenever I seen one in a field or someplace I always laughed at them so stupid lookin and cute, fuck—I never told the other guys they were there case they burn them or something. Anyways I try puttin pictures of these baby sheep overtop of the cauliflower and I'll do it and it's okay for a second then the lamb its eyes'll go all funny like slits lookin sideways just like them snakes and then it'll open its mouth and there'll be them long sharp teeth and a bunch of worms inside and the nice little sheep goes all ugly on

me and the cauliflower comes back worse than
ever like it ate the sheep or sornethin... Maybe
if I could just have a car or get back to workin on
cars, you know? Or get into Dragmasters, then
maybe I'd stop thinkin of these things. I don't
know. I'm lookin for somebody who knows, that's
why I'm askin youse, I don't know. I wish I did.
(*pause*) If it was in front of me I'd beat it to shit,
you know?

Act Two, Scene Two

> ALAN *and* THERESA *at home.* ALAN *comes in*
> *after work.* THERESA *is watching television,*
> *laughing.*

ALAN   Did ya do it, did ya get it done?

THERESA   You got somethin on your mouth ,Al.

ALAN   (*wipes*) What was it?

THERESA   Look like cream from one of them Jos. Louis.

ALAN   What I got on my face don't matter, Trese, I
            asked ya a question.

THERESA   What?

ALAN   Did ya get what I told ya done?

THERESA   Readin writin?

ALAN   Yes.

THERESA   Shhhh baby sleepin, Al.

ALAN   Did—let's see. Awwwww hey, Danny! He's not
              sleepin! Hey, ya little bugger, how ya doin—this
              is your dad—this is your dad speakin, ya know
              me? Hey? He does, he knows me. Don't ya,
              Danny. Hey, Danny, did your angel mummy do
              what Daddy asked her to? Eh? Yes? She did? Oh
              thank you, Danny, you are the most neatest cut-
              est little baby boy—what's that on his chin?

THERESA   From eatin milk.

ALAN   Theresa, you don't eat milk you drink it.

THERESA   I know.

ALAN   There. Wipe that ugly milk offa ya. Eh Danny?
              You are my little bugger and I'm your daddy!
              Hey! Your mummy gonna show me what she
              done! Okay, Mummy, now show me what ya
              done.

THERESA   I lost it.

ALAN   How could you lose it?

THERESA   I done it, Al, but I lost it.

ALAN   Theresa. Theresa, I'm gonna try not to get mad
              at ya but ya can't keep doin this to me! Every day
              you're tellin me ya lost your homework!

THERESA	Maybe someone take it.
ALAN	Theresa, don't you understand I am tryin to improve my family.
THERESA	*(coyly)* Al.
ALAN	What.
THERESA	*(delighted)* You shoulda seen the poo I done today, it was hardly long!
ALAN	Theresa, married ladies with babies ain't supposed to say things like that!
THERESA	Sorry.
ALAN	Danny could hear ya, ya know.
THERESA	I don't think he hear, Al, I think he deaf.
ALAN	What?
THERESA	I shoutin in his ear he don't do nothin.
ALAN	Trese, ya don't go shoutin in babies' ears!

THERESA kisses ALAN. He melts.

THERESA	I love ya, Al.
ALAN	You know I love you, don't ya, you know it— more than anything in this whole world, you and Danny boy.

THERESA   I know, Al. How many dishes you done today?

ALAN   Two hundred and twenty-three.

THERESA   Jeez.

ALAN   Yup. That's ten more than yesterday.

THERESA   Jeez.

Act Two, Scene Three

> THERESA *has been sleeping over at* SANDY's *because* SANDY *is scared. Cat scream.*

SANDY   What's that noise? Trese, wake up. Hear that?

THERESA   What?

SANDY   Listen—oh Jesus, what is it?

THERESA   Maybe it Charlie Manson.

SANDY   Oh shut up, you watch too much TV.

THERESA   Maybe it a pussy cat.

SANDY   Hello? Hello? Anybody there? Trese, hand me somethin. The lamp.

THERESA   Why?

SANDY   Shut your mouth and don't ask questions.

THERESA   Okay okay, here.

SANDY   Okay. You get the knife from the top drawer just
             in case he comes in here.

THERESA   Who, Charlie Manson?

SANDY   Don't say that name, Trese. Scream if anybody
             comes...

THERESA   I will, Sandy.

             SANDY *goes to the other room. She screams a
             primal scream.*

SANDY   (*returns*) It was nothin.

THERESA   How come.

SANDY   'Cause.

THERESA   How come my baby never smilin?

SANDY   Are ya doin what the workers tell ya?

THERESA   Al do it, he don't let me do nothin.

SANDY   Why?

THERESA   He smarter.

SANDY   I guess so.

THERESA	He love Danny. He wash him with soap and he feed him and he huggin him.
SANDY	What's he feedin him?
THERESA	Bologna.
SANDY	At four months?
THERESA	He love it.
SANDY	Oh Christ. Don't ya have baby food?
THERESA	I don't know.
SANDY	What am I gonna do with you?
THERESA	I'm glad I stayin here. Al cryin nights.
SANDY	How come?
THERESA	I don't know. I tell him nothin's wrong, everything fine, but he keep cryin.
SANDY	Trese, do ya think Joe'll come back?
THERESA	He proly comin back next Friday.
SANDY	If he do, he can go to hell.
THERESA	Bonnie Cain say he never comin back.
SANDY	She did?

THERESA   She don't know nothin. He comin back.

SANDY   I got a letter.

THERESA   Ya did?

SANDY   I burnt it though, didn't read it.

THERESA   Sandy, you depress?

SANDY   No. I just don't like stayin alone nights, it ain't good for ya.

THERESA   You could come stayin with us.

SANDY   Uh uh. No way. I don't want to see no baby eatin bologna.

THERESA   Oh.

SANDY   You get in some baby food, Trese, or I'm reporting ya to the social worker.

THERESA   Okay.

SANDY   Okay?

THERESA   I'm gonna.

SANDY   You go on to sleep. Now.

THERESA   Night, Sandy. Don't go havin no bad dreams.

SANDY   Night.

THERESA *falls asleep instantly.* SANDY *stays awake, staring out.*

Act Two, Scene Four

ALAN *has just been fired from his dishwashing job. He is thrown out of a door, real or imaginary, onto a busy street. He has stolen an egg, which he carries in his hand.*

ALAN   (*holding up egg as pointer*) I was quittin anyways, ya bastards, there's white worms in the hamburg, I seen em, there's white worms in the hamburg! (*more quietly, to himself*) I seen em wiggle — (*turning to audience, in threatening tones*) There wasn't no egg on that pan, sir, there wasn't no egg on that fry pan.

ALAN *stares at the audience for a moment, gets the idea to throw the egg at the door and turns very slowly toward the door. Then in a flash starts to throw the egg but instead cracks it over his head. He puts the shell in his pocket, sees somebody in the distance, sticks down his hair, leans onto the sewer and discovers the Indian* MAN *with a bottle.* ALAN *grabs it and takes a sip.*

MAN   Man, who is standing between two girly-girls in the whirly-burl.

ALAN   Oh why don't ya just shut up...

MAN	*(pointing at constellation in the sky)* Double devil—stuck together—cha cha cha!
	JOE *appears, wearing a new coat and a hat that says "*SUCCESS*." ALAN rushes to greet him. By the end of the scene, they reach the entrance to* SANDY's *apartment.*
ALAN	Jesus, Joe! Joe! Hey, Joe, how're ya doin?
JOE	Hey, buddy, how are you?
ALAN	Okay, you know, hangin on. You—when did ya get back?
JOE	Just now, buddy, but not for long. I'm moving Sandy out there with me.
ALAN	No kidding? It's pretty good out there?
JOE	It's a great place, man, lots of work, nice people. Hell of a lot better than this hole, I'm tellin you.
ALAN	Yeah? Does Sandy know you're back?
JOE	Nope. I'm gonna surprise her. She'll be happy as hell to see me. Then the two of us are gonna take right off.
ALAN	That right? …Hey me and Theresa got a kid—a little boy, Danny.
JOE	Is that right? Danny, huh? So how do you like bein a father?

ALAN   It's all right, man. I like it. I make a good father I guess.

JOE   Yeah? …Well, I better head off.

ALAN   Hey—Joe—I got somethin to tell ya.

JOE   Is this a long story or a short one?

ALAN   Not too long—d'ju hear about Boyd's GTO?

JOE   What, the one that used to be parked on Johnson below Division?

ALAN   Yeah, you know, green with chrome mags and chrome cut-outs.

JOE   Yeah. What a fuckin beast. What about it?

ALAN   He totalled it.

JOE   Hah. Well it was a shitty-lookin car anyways.

ALAN   Yeah but fuck it had—it had them high-lift cam solid lifters, and, and high-compression kit and—

JOE   You name it.

ALAN   He had it. Yup. Hey—did you know it had four fuckin carbs?

JOE   Eat shit.

ALAN   No kiddin, four! But you know how come he
         kept it lookin so shitty?

JOE   Beats me.

ALAN   So the cops wouldn't notice. They all knew,
         though, eh, they knew what he had. Fuck that
         thing was fast, he used to shoot the main drag
         doin one-fifty.

JOE   Yeah? That's fast.

ALAN   Fuckin fast. You know how he totalled it?

JOE   No.

ALAN   Fuck it was funny. We were gettin polluted up
         at the Manor, eh, and Alfie decides he's gon-
         na go up to Gan. He was about half pissed I
         guess. So parently he tries to pass three or four
         cars same time except one of em happens to be
         a truck goin left. So I guess he almost makes
         it but the truck catches him by his back right
         fender and spins him. Huh. Flipped the car six
         fuckin times.

JOE   Jeez. How is he?

ALAN   Alfie? He's okay now but he got stabbed in
         the heart with the rear-view mirror. Had an
         operation.

JOE   That right?

ALAN	Chuck was with him and—
JOE	The Scotty?
ALAN	Yeah and he just jumped out and never even had a scratch on him. What's that, a present for the wife?
JOE	Yeah. That Charlie perfume shit.
ALAN	Hardly nice. Yeah, that's nice stuff. Women— they like that kinda stuff.
JOE	I know. Smells shitty to me.
ALAN	Yeah.
JOE	Well I gotta move, buddy, catch you later.
ALAN	Hey! Hey!

From his pocket ALAN *takes an ornamental iron monk with an erection. It is wrapped in newspaper.*

Here.

JOE	What's this?
ALAN	Just somethin.
JOE	Oh yeah. I seen one of these. Well I'm gone.
ALAN	See ya… Bye Joe!

Act Two, Scene Five

SANDY *and* JOE *seated at a table.*

SANDY   I got a fucking hole in my gut 'cause of you.

JOE   Who told ya that?

SANDY   Doctor Scott.

JOE   He don't know what he's talking about.

SANDY   Hurtin me all the time I had pain.

JOE   Not no more. Not no more ya won't.

SANDY   I was takin pills even—prescription!

JOE   I told ya, babe, I feel bad.

SANDY   I never done nothin to you. Why?

JOE   Ewwww Christ I missed your body, there was times I wanted ya so bad I could taste ya. I'd lie in bed there and think about you and what ya looked like stripped naked, think about your nice titties.

SANDY   Two old bags.

JOE   *Nothin*, them are peaches.

SANDY   Bullshit. I'm not goin back with ya.

JOE   Yes you are.

SANDY   Can't push me around no more.

JOE   Come on, just try it a couple weeks, if ya don't
           like it you can fuck off.

SANDY   Won't be nothin different.

JOE   It's gotta be different.

SANDY   It'll be the same as before, beatin up on me.

JOE   No way.

SANDY   How the fuck do I know?

JOE   'Cause it's fuckin true, that's how.

SANDY   I hate you. I hated you all the time you was gone.

JOE   I know.

SANDY   I woulda laughed if you hadda died.

JOE   I never did.

SANDY   I know.

JOE   So.

                   Pause.

SANDY   How come ya want me back.

JOE   Don't know. It's dog shit when you're gone.

SANDY   Then why'd ya stay so long.

JOE   Shit, Sandy.

SANDY   I was up nights shakin.

JOE   Scared of the crackwalker were ya?

SANDY   He never hurt nobody.

JOE   I missed makin it with ya. Did ya miss it with me?

SANDY   I didn't have no one.

JOE   That's 'cause you're mine.

SANDY   Is that right.

JOE   *(opens her gift)* Here. Smell that.

SANDY   Hmmn.

JOE   You told me you like that shit.

SANDY   It's okay.

JOE   Soooo. You been workin for Nikos?

SANDY   Some.

JOE   What else you been doin?

SANDY	Learned how to make a new drink.
JOE	What, rum and Coke?
SANDY	That's not new.
JOE	What, dough brain.
SANDY	A Dirty Mother, asshole.
JOE	A dirty mother asshole, what's that?
SANDY	A Dirty Mother! It's tequila, crème de cacao, and milk. It's hardly good.
JOE	Sounds like a chocky milkshake from Mexico.
SANDY	Arsewipe. I got a batch made up in the fridge, you want one?
JOE	Yeah, okay. I'll try one. Gimme a beer with it though.
SANDY	*(she goes to the kitchen; from kitchen)* You should give Al a call, he's in a bad way.
JOE	Yeah I seen him, he looked like shit.
SANDY	They got a kid, Danny.
JOE	He was tellin me.
SANDY	It's a medical retard.

JOE   Fuuuuck.

SANDY   It don't ever move its face—like a doll.

JOE   See this thing he give me?

SANDY   What is it?

JOE   I don't know. An iron monk with a hard-on?

SANDY   Jeez, where'd he get that, up at Van's?

JOE   I guess so. (SANDY *brings ina tray.*) Well fuckin
            jumpqueen, eh, where'd ya get them glasses?

SANDY   My girlfriend Gail, she scoffed em offa the 401
            Inn.

JOE   Fuckin eh.

SANDY   They'd cost ya, ya know.

JOE   Hmmm. That's, ahhh that's a shit-hot drink.

SANDY   Me and Gail drink it all the time when we go
            out.

JOE   It's not bad.

SANDY   We always order it, only none of em knows how
            to make it, so we have to tell them.

JOE   Yeah?

SANDY	I can make any kind of drink now she taught me.
JOE	What're you doin, two women goin drinkin alone together.
SANDY	Who said we were alone?
JOE	Come here.
SANDY	Joe, it ain't like that no more.
JOE	Who said it ain't.
SANDY	I did. Keep your paws offa me.
JOE	Jeez you're lookin good.
SANDY	I'm doin my eyeliner different.
JOE	Yeah?
SANDY	Makes my eyes look bigger.
JOE	Nice.
SANDY	I know.

Act Two, Scene Six

> ALAN *and* THERESA's *place.* THERESA *is playing with the baby. There are tea things set out.*

> *The baby does not respond to anything. The crib is offstage.*

THERESA   Beebeebeebee... How come you not drinkin
your tea, beebee? You got a bad cold? Poor beebee. *(singing)* My little baby is my baby my little Danny is my angel baby I take care of him,
and he don't cry or nothin and he ain't never
gonna have the crib death neither— *(speaking)* No way, Danny, 'cause I love ya. Al loves
ya too but he a bastard sometime, I know he
don't talk nice in front of you sometime—don't
you go goin into one of them deep sleeps, beebee—no—hey! Hey, baby Danny! Wake up
'cause that's how them other babies got the crib
death! From sleepin too deep! S'true! You darlin little baby! You mine! That sosha worker's
hardly nice, eh? Look! *(dangles Jos. Louis wrap-
per in front of Danny)* Look at that, baby, you
like that? Eh? It's hardly pretty! You come on,
come on, gimme a smile, beebee; you thinkin
too much, just like Al, that why you so serious
all the time. Ohhhhh baby *(She rocks him.)*
so soff. Skin hardly soff. Hey! I look like that
Madonna lady and she holdin baby Jesus just
like I holdin you so you mus look like Jesus!
Baby Jesus! Oooohhh, Danny, you my beebee
Jesus and I the Madonna lady and Al, maybe
he Joseph, he make stuff outta wood. You like a
little horsey made outta wood, carry you down
Princess Street when we go to the s&r? I love
ya, beebee. That a little smile? Oh! Oh baby
baby Jesus I love ya!

ALAN   *(comes blasting through the door, starts tearing
                up the place—medicine, creams, clothes, every-
                thing)* No fuckin social worker's gonna fuckin
                tell me how to run my fuckin life! I don't take
                this fuckin shit from nobody! Nobody don't tell
                me what to do and nobody don't tell me how to
                take care of my baby never! That means you too,
                you fuckin woman—I'm not takin any shit from
                you neither! There. We're not using any of their
                cocksucking medicine—they'll try to kill you
                with it!

THERESA   Al! Al, stop it!

ALAN   They did, they killed my dad with all their fuckin
                medicine! He didn't have no hair and he didn't
                have no flesh, just bones all over and ugly and
                yellow. No way, Therese, no way you could stop
                me, I'm throwin it all fuckin out! Out the win-
                dow, watch! There! It's out the window! Danny!
                Hey, Danny, my boy, my own son see? You don't
                have to be takin any of that ugly tastin shit no
                more!

THERESA   But he gonna get numona if he don't take his
                medicine, doctor say so! Nurse say he hafta take
                it three time a day or he gettin worse! Doctor
                sees you done that he won't give us no more
                medicine for Danny! You basard! You basard!
                (She hits him.)

ALAN   Arsewipe! Don't you know nothin? Don't you
                know them doctors make money offa sick ba-
                bies? That's why they like to keep em sick with

	all them medicines! So they make more fuckin money!
THERESA	I don't believe ya. Doctors are nice, they wouldn't go makin babies sick!
ALAN	Jeez you're a dumbrain sometimes, Therese, they don't give a fuck about our fuckin baby so long as they get their TVs and golf clubs and that. They care dick! That's why they give em this poison so the baby stay sick!
THERESA	It not poison, it good for ya, the nurse say so! She don't even have no TV, she tole me. So you're crazy, I know that stuff good for Danny, he gettin better already!
ALAN	That baby ain't gettin no better, you stupid woman, you know it ain't. It looks strange. It don't look right and that's 'cause they're givin it all them fuckin medicines! Fuck them! So no more!
THERESA	Really would them doctors do that? Really?
ALAN	Fuckin right they would. Bastards.
THERESA	Bastards. How come? How come they hurtin my little baby?
ALAN	Money. Money and bucks. Cocksuckers.
THERESA	Well what we gonna do about all his snifflin and that?

ALAN   Well I know what to do, the social worker even
              said I did. He said I was a great father and you
              even heard him. I was a great father.

THERESA   S'true, Alan.

ALAN   Well, it got a cold, right? So if ya got a cold, ya
              gotta get warm, what else? It's fuckin simple and
              them doctors always do everything to make it
              harder! Fuck! So all we do, is ahh—turn on the
              oven! It's easy! Here. Put it to about five hun-
              dred—there—and open the door like that—
              and—now bring him over—

THERESA   Why? What you gonna do?

ALAN   Just bring the baby over, Trese. Do what I tell ya!

THERESA   Al, you not cooking the baby, are ya? *(weeping
              with confusion)*

ALAN   *(laughs)* Huh. Wait'll I tell Joe that, he'll laugh.
              Cookin the baby. Right. Jesus, arsehole, it's just
              like at the farm back in Picton when Mum used
              to sit by the stove with Ronny to warm him up,
              that's all! It's easy! If a guy's got a cold, warm him
              up!

THERESA   Oh. Don't make it too hot though.

ALAN   Keep out of it, woman. *(brings baby close to the
              stove)* There. There ya go, Danny! How you doin
              anyways, you little bugger—that's right, it's your

daddy, he come to make you better! Getcha away from all them fuckin doctors! That's right.

THERESA   Al, he's coughin! Can't we get back some of that cough syrup?

ALAN   Listen, stupid, we're not usin any of that stuff, I told ya! Didn't ya hear me or what? Listen. If he's coughin we'll just get that Vicks vapour rub that my old man used to use.

THERESA   That stuff smell too much!

ALAN   If it's good enough for my old man it's good enough for my baby, Therese. He used to put it all over his chest and his cough be gone the nex day. Here.

> *He puts a whole jar of Vicks over the baby's body.*

THERESA   Al, you puttin too much!

ALAN   Don't tell me what to do! Shut up! I know what I'm doin, I told ya the social worker said I was a great father! So shut up!

There. You're gonna be just fine now, baby.

THERESA   Al, you sure it ain't too much.

ALAN   Shhhhh. He's goin to sleep. Come here. I got somethin for ya.

THERESA   You did? What'dja get, doughnuts?

ALAN   *(He hands the baby to* THERESA *and opens the perfume—orange, cheap, and broken in the package.)* Shit. It broke on me. It's okay though, here I'll put it in a glass. *(He does so.)* There. *(hands it to her, takes the baby and puts him on a blanket or in a baby rocker on the floor)*

THERESA   Smell that. That's hardly beautiful, Al. Thank you, I love perfume.

ALAN   I know ya do. Ya like it?

THERESA   I love it. It hardly smells nice.

ALAN   *(caresses her)* Guess why I brung it?

THERESA   Why?

ALAN   I love you and you're my angel Madonna.

THERESA   A-l-l-l-l-l.

ALAN   It's true. Come here, angel. Hey. Ehhey. You know I love makin love to ya. I love fuckin you and chewin ya out. *(whispers)* I do.

THERESA   I know.

        ALAN *starts to undress her. They start necking on the floor next to the baby.* THERESA *stops suddenly.*

Oh oh.

ALAN   What?

THERESA   We can't do it, Al.

ALAN   Don't matter if you're bleedin.

THERESA   No I can't do it till I get my new IUD in. Or I get pregnant again, doctor say so!

ALAN   Fuck the goddamn doctors! Goddamn doctors trying to run my life, saying I can't make love to my own woman, to my own wife, fuck em fuck em. I don't care if you get pregnant, we're gonna do it when we want and no doctor's gonna tell us nothin.

THERESA   No! No, Alan, please! Get off me, you bastard, we're not doin it today no way! No! Get offa me or I callin the cops.

ALAN   *(He hits her, sends her across the room.)* You stupid dumb cunt Indian bitch face fat fat retarded whore. I don't want ya anyways! *(He collapses on the floor, now meeker, almost whiney.)* Alls I wanted was a little lovin anyways, there's nothin wrong with that? A man is sposda get lovin from his woman, ain't he? That is how come ya get married, ain't it? All I wanted was a little lovin, that's all… that's alllll.

The baby is crying.

Look what you done, woman, you makin the baby cry! You stupid bitch!

THERESA gets up to go to the baby.

No! No you stay down, I'm the only one who can make him stop cryin. Watch. Hey baby. Hey baby, here's your daddy. He's a great daddy, huh? Eh?

The baby is screaming.

THERESA   Take it away from the stove, Alan! Take it away from the stove!

ALAN takes the baby offstage to his crib.

ALAN   *(to THERESA)* Shhhhh. *(to baby)* Come on, baby, stop that cryin, Daddy don't like it when you cryin! Shhhh. Now shhhhhh. Gonna buy you a car when you get older—what kind you want, a Monte Carlo? Okay. I'm gonna get you a Monte Carlo. You wait, I'm gonna get work in a station and I'm gonna buy my own and I'm gonna get you anything you want. Okay? Now shhhhhhh. Stop cryin, I'm gonna get you a Monte Carlo, didn't ya hear me? Didn't ya? Shhhhhh. Be quiet, your mum is tryin to sleep, okay? Shhhhhh! Come on, come on. My little Danny boy baby. Come onnnn. Shhhhhhhh!

> *The baby cries and cries and cries while ALAN is talking, but finally, on the last "Shhhhh," is totally silent; suffocated, not deliberately, by ALAN. ALAN is now in a fugue state. He*

> *appears on stage, very wooden, like a sleep-walker. Looks at* THERESA, *who is watching in wonder.*

It's okay. It's okay, it's not cryin anymore. See. It's quiet now. It's not cryin. I—I—I done it, see? See? I'm a good father, he—you know how come he stopped? 'Cause I told him he was gonna get a Monte Carlo.

THERESA   What's that?

ALAN   It's a kind of car. It's a place too. One of them south-sea islands. Maybe we'll go there, eh? Anyways I gotta g,o I gotta meet somebody... see ya.

> ALAN *goes.* THERESA *looks after him.*

Act Two, Scene Seven

> JOE *and* SANDY's. ALAN, JOE *and* SANDY *are watching a Leafs hockey game on television.* ALAN *is sitting away from* JOE *and* SANDY, *and he is smoking and loudly eating barbecue chips.* JOE *and* SANDY *are very much involved with each other and the game and they virtually ignore* ALAN.

JOE   Go go go, you fucker—Bunnyfuck, what are you fuckin doin—*get him off Nykoluk, get him off the ice, fuck.*

ALAN   Imlach dies.

            JOE does not respond.

            IMLACH DIES!

JOE   Oh LAROUQUE—come on, Sittler, put that
            mother in, come on come on, FUCK OFF,
            PERRAULT, do it, Daryl, hey Martin Martin, put
            it in put it, ALL RIGHT! *(jumps up)* ALL FUCKING
            RIGHT!

            *ALAN jumps up with JOE, leans into the TV,
            his face only one inch away from the screen,
            screams, wagging his head.*

ALAN   ALLLLL FUCKIN RIGHT!

            Looks back at JOE with a little laugh.

SANDY   *(jocularly)* Take a bird, why don't ya?

            ALAN continues yelling into the TV.

JOE   Hey, Al, don't scare the TV away he—

            *THERESA appears in the doorany with a bag in
            her hand. She is reminiscent of Cassandra in
            The Trojan Women.*

THERESA   YOU TOLE HIM YOU GIVE HIM A MONTE CARLO AND
            YA DON'T EVEN DRIVE ONE. YA DON'T EVEN DRIVE
            ONE.

Her presence is so strong that she immediate-ly captures their attention.

I not goin screwin with ya no more, Al, no way. No way! You stoppem breathin. I tell him, "Breathin, baby, breathin," and he not 'cause *you stoppenim.*

ALAN   *(looking away from* THERESA*)* She's lyin, you guys, stop your lyin.

THERESA   You goin up the river to Penetang, Al, you goin there tomorrow and you never comin out for what you done, you not goin back with me, I goin with Ron Harton, he better than you, he not stoppem breathin, he still livin up on Division up at Shuter's? I callin him up and I goin steady with him, he better lookin, you funny lookin, I screwin him.

ALAN   YOU lyin fat COW, you don't know what you're fuckin talkin about, crazy fucking whorebag—LIAR!

            ALAN *knocks* THERESA *to the floor, hesitates, grabs two glasses half-full of Dirty Mother and runs off.* JOE *follows.*

THERESA   You got a doughnut, Sanny, gimme a donut.

SANDY   What have ya got in the bag, Trese.

THERESA   Ivy, Ivy gimme the bag, I not givin it.

SANDY   What's in it, though.

THERESA   I takin him up the graveyard.

SANDY   What for.

THERESA   I puttin him with Grandma down St. Mary's, Sanny, see ya later.

SANDY   *(stepping in front of* THERESA'*s exit)* Wait a minute, what—

THERESA   Fuck off, Sandy.

SANDY   What's inside it.

     THERESA *giggles.* SANDY *touches the bag, flinches.*

     I'm callin the cops.

THERESA   Agghhhhh. You fuckin call anyone, I takin one of my fits.

SANDY   I'm shakin in my shoes, Trese. *(begins to dial)*

THERESA   *(grabs* SANDY, *rips phone from the wall)* You not callin—

SANDY   *(gets up, begins to exit, turns around, points at* THERESA*)* You're not here when I get back and I'm tellin Ron Harton what ya done down the Lido, ya hear me?

     THERESA *stares at* SANDY *in horror.*

I will, too.

THERESA   Okay.

SANDY   I mean it. *(exits)*

THERESA   *(to baby in bag)* It okay, Danny, don't you be cr-
            yin now, you with baby Jesus sittin on the cloud
            and the Virgin lookin like me, she with ya, she
            sittin there wearin that long blue dress goin
            down to her feet hardly pretty, eh? ...Danny?
            You still live? You breathin if I breathin into
            ya? S'okay I'm your mum! *(tries to breathe into
            baby)* Danny? You dead, eh? You not live. You
            never comin back, eh. *(puts bag to side, picks up
            the severed phone, does not dial)* Hi Janus, won't
            be doin readin writin today. Somethin happen.
            Just somethin. The baby die. The baby die. Up
            at Sanny's. Okay okay I waitin... Ron Harton
            still livin up at Shuter's? *(hangs up the phone
            and picks it up immediately)* C'I speak to Ron,
            please? Hi Ron, its Trese. S'okay if we start goin
            together, I love ya. Okay, see ya Tuesday.

            SANDY *enters, breathless, leans against the
            door. She cannot look at* THERESA.

SANDY   Don't want you tellin no stories to the cops, you
            hear me? Want you to tell em the truth exactly
            like it happened, okay?

THERESA   Don't like ya no more, Sanny.

SANDY   S'too bad.

THERESA   You a dirty faggot.

SANDY   Right.

THERESA   Not my friend no more!

SANDY   Okay...

THERESA   I not talkin to YOU.

           She turns her back to SANDY. *She is crying.*
           SANDY *notices.*

SANDY   You should come out to Calgary sometime — visit.

THERESA   No, Sanny, I workin!

SANDY   What?

THERESA   *(tells story joyously with no trace of grief)* Down
           at Kresge's up with Ivy. Hah! She hardly funny,
           she hardly get pissed off when I eatin icin, she
           yellin, "Trese, if you eat one more chocolate icin
           I tellin Charlie," so I go, "You tellin Charlie I
           tellin on you, Ivy, snitchin butter tarts!" They're
           hardly good, though, them tarts. Ivy English...
           Sorry I can't comin with ya out west, Sanny...
           Ivy be piss off.

Act Two, Scene Eight

> ALAN *and Indian* MAN *on a warm air vent.* ALAN
> *is leaning against a wall. He is clanging two*
> *glasses together. This produces a spooky sound.*

ALAN (*pointing to* MAN) You fuckin touch me and I'll
break your head.

MAN Hee hee hee Church'n Mondee all dee Mondee
hee hee hee!

ALAN I will break your fuckin head in!

MAN (*starts happily, becomes angry as he remembers*
incident with a paramedic who denied him phe-
nobarbital) Breakin my fa fa pheno phenobarbi-
doll—barbidoll—NIGGER, YOU NIGGER!

ALAN Shut it, you fuck, just shut it.

> MAN *in panic rushes toward the audience.*

MAN SHUT THE WINDOW, SHUT THE WINDOW, SHUT THE
WINDOW… (*laughs*)

ALAN Nothing's funny, okay, so—just—STOP LAUGHIN.
Just pass out, will ya, can't ya just pass out? (MAN
vomits on ALAN's *sock.*) Ahhhh fuck you goddamn
shit. SHIT! Eccchh you keep your puke to yourself, you old fuck! (*crouches, rocking*) I could
drive a Monte Carlo, I know I could. (*rubbing*
glasses together)

JOE enters looking for ALAN, *spots him, then crosses to him.*

JOE   Al?

ALAN   Joe!

JOE   Look—ah—

ALAN   She's lyin, Joe, I could drive a Monte Carlo.

JOE   Al?

ALAN   I could drive one easy.

JOE   You could drive any car on the road. Now why don't you come on—

ALAN   I—I—I can't.

JOE   Why not?

ALAN   I—I—I'm too cold, you know? I'm freezin.

JOE   You're okay, ya probably got a flu, ya got a bug, okay?

ALAN   No, no, I don't got a bug, I'm just cold, he puked on me.

JOE   So he puked on ya, Martin used to puke on ya all the time. Come on—come on out of that shit pit and I'll get ya a coffee.

ALAN   NO. No, I don't want to, I just don't want to, okay?

JOE   Suit yourself. *(turns his back on* ALAN, *starts to leave)*

ALAN   I done what I done and I done it and I fucked it up so I'm payin for it, get it? I'm payin for it.

JOE   I don't know what ya done.

ALAN   Sorry, Joe.

            JOE *looks at him, can't think of what to say.*

            Joe.

JOE   Yeah.

ALAN   Could ya do one thing?

JOE   What.

ALAN   Tell her I could drive a Monte Carlo. Easy.

JOE   I will.

ALAN   Bye, Joe. *(crouches in previous position, zipping and unzipping his jacket)* "Nobody here—but us chickens—nobody here but us guys—don't bother me we got work to do and eggs to lay— and guys to see—"

MAN   SHHHHHHHHHHHHHhhhhhhhhh. *(with no motion, just the sound)*

Act Two, Scene Nine

SANDY   I think it's better off dead. I'm not kiddin ya, I'm
             serious. It don't hurt babies to be dead, they go
             straight on up to heaven, no hell no purgatory
             no nothin no problems. 'Cause their souls are
             still white as snow—they ain't had the time to get
             them black and ugly. Not like the rest of us—oh
             no, if a baby dies he's just fine, he don't even know
             he's dead. Youse shoulda seen him lyin there in
             that casket he looked fine. They had them little
             pyjamas on him Trese got up at the s&r, the ones
             with all them dogs chasin cats all over, all yel-
             low? They hardly looked sweet. And they had a
             big wreath of flowers around his neck so's to hide
             the strangle—you know the kind you put on your
             door at Christmas? Like that. It was kinda nice.
             We all lined up to take a look at him too—first
             time he got so much attention in his life—no-
             body broke up or nothin, not even Trese. In fact
             I was scared she was gonna break up laughin. I'm
             not kiddin ya, it don't bug her at all the kid's gone.
             Jeez y'know I don't know what goes on inside that
             girl but it ain't what's goin on inside the rest of us.
             She only got one thing on her mind now, that's
             goin after Ron Harton. Don't ask me why, he
             looks like the fucking wrath of God. He's a pig
             too. I don't blame Trese though, I still feel for her
             even—fuck—this old bag sittin behind me was
             goin on about how come Trese never went to the
             hairdressers, you know what her hair is like, eh,
             right in the middle of the service, so I turn around
             and I says, "You're gonna hardly think of goin to

the hairdressers when your own baby's just been killed by your own husband, ya fuckin old hag." I called her that too, right to her face. Oh yeah I'll stand up for a friend, anytime. I'll tell ya who else I stood up for at that service... Al, and he done it. Oh yeah, I still consider him a friend. No matter what he done, nobody can say what happened in that room; so I walk into the funeral parlour, and I take one of them cookies they got lyin out, you know, just tea biscuits, and I turn around and who's standin behind me lookin me right in the eye but that goddamn Bonnie Cain. She comes up close, her breath just reekin, and she says to me how she seen the whole thing from the window and how he done it with a plastic bag, one of them Glad Bags, and how Trese was lookin on and laughin. That goddamn holy bitch. "You lie," I says to her and I grab her by the tit and I says, "You fuckin houndog, one more word outta you and I send you to your goddamn grave..." He never done it with a plastic bag, he done it with his hands. I woulda, I woulda broke every bone in her fuckin body and she knowed it too. She didn't say nothin more. Jeez I'll be glad to get outta this hole, I'm tellin ya. I won't miss it neither, I won't even dream about it. I won't. I worry about Trese but she'll be okay, you know? She'll—she'll go back down the Lido, start blowin off old queers again for five bucks. It's still open, it won't never close... They had them flowers round Danny's neck so's to hide the strangle but I seen it. The flowers never hid it, they just made ya look harder, ya know? They just made ya look harder.

Act Two, Scene Ten

Small struggle offstage. THERESA *runs on stage.*

THERESA   Stupid old bassard, don't go foolin with me, you don't even know who I look like even. You don't even know who I lookin like.

Original Act Two, Scene Six

> ALAN *and* THERESA's *place. One room. Maybe bachelor. Messy. Small* TV *on. Baby crib in the middle of the room. A prominent shelf with pills, diapers, stuff provided by the public health nurse and parent aids (bright things, etc., learning aids). Place is dingy.*

> THERESA *is playing with the baby. They are having a cup of tea together. The baby is motionless. An obvious doll with staring eyes should be used.*

THERESA   Bebebebebe… How come you not drinkin your tea, beebee? *(song, tune made up)* My little baby is my baby my little Danny is my angel baby I take care of him, and he don't cry or nothin, and he ain't never gonna have the crib death neither— *(speech)* No way, Danny, 'cause I love ya. Al loves ya too but he a bastard sometime, I know he don't talk nice in front of you sometime—don't you go goin into one of them deep sleeps, beebee—no—hey! Hey, baby Danny? Wake up 'cause that's how them other babies got the crib death! From sleepin too deep! S'true! You darlin little beebee! You mine! That sosha worker's hardly nice, eh? Look! *(she takes one of the bright-coloured objects and dangles it in front of his face)* Look at that, baby, you like that? It's hardly pretty! You come on, come gimme a smile, baby—you thinkin too much, just like Al, that why you so serious alls the time. Ohhhhh baby. *(She rocks it.)* So soff. Skin hardly soff. Hey! *(in tiny voice)* I look like that Madonna lady and she holdin baby Jesus jus like I holdin you so you mus look like Jesus! Baby Jesus! Oooohhh, Danny, you my beebee Jesus and I the Madonna lady and Al, maybe he Joseph. He make stuff outta wood. You like a little horsey made outta wood, carry you down Princess Street when we go to the S&R? I love ya, beebee. That a little smile? Oh! Oh baby baby Jesus I love ya!

> *Suddenly,* ALAN *comes tearing in, bag in hand, goes straight for the pill and gaily coloured object shelf, and knocks the whole thing down. Then he starts to pick up each salve and bottle and destroy everything. As he does this, he says the following:*

ALAN

No fuckin social worker's gonna fuckin tell me how to run my fuckin life! I don't take this fuckin shit from nobody! Nobody don't tell me what to do and nobody don't tell me how to take care of my baby never! That means you too, you fuckin woman, I'm not takin any shit from you neither! There. We're not using any of their cocksuckin medicine—they'll try to kill you with it!

THERESA   Al! Al, stop it!

ALAN   They did, they killed my dad with all their fuck-
              ing medicine! He didn't have no hair and he
              didn't have no flesh, just bones all over and ugly
              and yellow and crazy and right out of his mind,
              he went 'cause of their fuckin medicine! No way,
              Therese, no way you could stop me, I'm throwin
              it all fuckin out! Out the window, watch! *(He
              does.)* There! It's out the window! Danny! Hey,
              Danny, my boy, my own son see? You don't have
              to be takin any of that ugly tastin stuff no more!

THERESA   But he gonna get numona if he don't take his
              medicine, doctor say so! Nurse say he hafta take
              it three time a day or he gettin worse! Alan! You
              basard, you throwin out all that medicine they
              givin us, what you gonna do for him? He snifflin
              and coughing and that and he can't even hardly
              breathin sometimes? Doctor sees you done that
              he won't give us no more medicine for Danny!
              You basard! You basard! *(She hits him weakly, he
              has a sort of fake calm now.)*

ALAN   Arsewipe! Don't you know nothin? Don't you
              know them doctors make money offa sick ba-
              bies? That's why they like to keep em sick with
              all them medicines! So they make more fuckin
              money!

THERESA   I don't believe ya. Doctors are nice, they wouldn't
              go makin babies sick!

ALAN   Jeez you're a dumbrain sometimes, Trese. They
              don't give a fuck about our fuckin baby so long as
              they get their TVs and golf clubs and that. They

care dick! That's why they give em this poison so the baby stay sick!

THERESA   It not poison, it good for ya, the nurse say so! She don't even have no TV. She tole me. So you're crazy, I know that stuff good for Danny, he gettin better already! Why you go throwin it out? Bastard.

ALAN   That baby ain't gettin no better, you stupid woman, you know it ain't. It looks strange. It don't look right and that's 'cause they're givin it all them fuckin medicines! Fuck them! So no more!

THERESA   Really would them doctors do that? Really?

ALAN   Fuckin right they would. Bastards.

THERESA   Bastards. How come? How come they hurtin my little baby?

ALAN   Money. Money and bucks. Cocksuckers.

THERESA   Well what we gonna do about all his snifflin and that? Poor little thing, he all stuffed up.

ALAN   Well I know what to do, the social worker even said I did. He said I was a great father and you even heard him. I was a great father.

THERESA   S'true, Alan.

ALAN   Well, it got a cold, right? So if ya got a cold, ya gotta get warm, what else? It's fuckin simple and them doctors always do everything to make it harder! Fuck! So alls we do, is ahh—turn on the oven! It's easy! Here. Put it to about five hundred—there—and open the door like that—and—now bring him over—

THERESA   Why? What you gonna do?

ALAN   Just bring the baby over, Trese. Do what I tell ya!

THERESA   Al, you not cooking the baby, are ya? *(weeping with confusion)*

ALAN   *(laughs)* Huh. Wait'll I tell Joe that, he'll laugh. Cookin the baby. Right. Jesus, arsehole, it's just like at the farm back in Picton when Mum used to sit by the stove with Ronny to warm him up, that's all! It's easy! If a guy's got a cold, warm him up!

THERESA   Oh. Don't make it too hot though.

ALAN   Keep out of it, woman. *(places the crib as close to the stove as he can get it)* There. There ya go, Danny! How you doin anyways, you little bugger—that's right, it's your daddy, he come to make you better! Getcha away from all them fuckin doctors! That's right.

THERESA   Al, he's coughin! Can't we get back some of that cough syrup?

ALAN   Listen, stupid, we're not usin any of that stuff, I told ya! Didn't ya hear me or what? Listen. If he's coughin we'll just get that Vicks vapour rub that my old man used to use.

THERESA   That stuff smell too much!

ALAN   If it's good enough for my old man it's good enough for my baby, Therese. He used to put it all over his chest and his cough be gone the nex day. Here.

    He puts a whole jar of Vicks over the baby's body.

THERESA   Al, you puttin too much!

ALAN   Don't tell me what to do! Shut up! I know what I'm doin, I told ya the social worker said I was a great father! So shut up!

    He holds the baby up. It is glistening with the stuff.

There. You're gonna be just fine now, baby.

THERESA   Al, you sure it ain't too much.

ALAN   Shhhhh. He's goin to sleep. Come here. I got somethin for ya.

THERESA   You did? What'dja get, doughnuts?

ALAN   *(opens perfume—orange, cheap, and it has broken in the package)* Shit. It broke on me. It's okay though, here I'll put it in a glass. *(He does so.)* There. *(hands it to her)*

THERESA   Smell that. That's hardly beautiful, Al. Thank you, I love perfume.

ALAN   I know ya do. Ya like it?

THERESA   I love it. Hardly smells nice.

ALAN   *(starts coming on to her)* Guess why I brung it?

THERESA   Why?

ALAN   I love you and you're my angel Madonna.

THERESA   Alllll.

ALAN   It's true. Come here, angel. Hey. Ehyey. You know I love makin love to ya. I love fuckin you and chewin ya out. *(whispers)* I do.

THERESA   I know.

ALAN   *(starts to undress her)* Come on. Oh jeez you make me horny. Look, he's hard as anything.

> *They start necking on the floor next to the baby, then* THERESA *stops suddenly.*

THERESA   Uh oh.

ALAN   What?

THERESA	We can't do it, Al.
ALAN	Don't matter if you're bleedin.
THERESA	No, I can't do it till I get my new IUD in. Or I get pregnant again, doctor say so!
ALAN	Fuck the goddamn doctors! *(flings her away or something)* Goddamn doctors trying to run my life, sayin I can't make love to my own woman, to my own wife, fuck em fuck em fuck em. Come here, we're gonna do it anyways and I don't care if you get pregnant, we're gonna do it when we want and no doctor's gonna tell us nothin.
THERESA	No! No, Alan, please! Get off me, you bastard, we're not doin it today no way! No! Get offa me or I callin the cops.
ALAN	*(He hits her, sends her across the room.)* You stupid dumb cunt Indian bitch face fat fat retarded whore. I don't want ya anyways! *(He collapses on the floor, now meeker, almost whiney.)* Alls I wanted was a little lovin anyways—there's nothin wrong with that? A man is sposda get lovin from his woman, ain't he? That is how come ya get married, ain't it? All I wanted was a little lovin, that's all… that's alllll.

The baby is crying.

Look what you done, woman, you makin the baby cry! You stupid bitch!

THERESA gets up to go to the baby.

No! No you stay down, I'm the only one who can make him stop cryin. Watch. Hey baby. Hey baby, here's your daddy. He's a great daddy, huh? Eh?

The baby is screaming.

THERESA   Take it away from the stove, Alan! Take it away from the stove!

ALAN   *(to THERESA)* Shhhhh. *(to baby)* Come on, baby, stop that cryin, Daddy don't like it when you cryin! Shhhh. Now shhhhhh! Gonna buy you a car when you get older—what kind you want, a Monte Carlo? Okay. I'm gonna get you a Monte Carlo. You wait. I'm gonna get work in a station and I'm gonna buy my own and I'm gonna get you anything you want. Okay? Now shhhhhhhh. Stop cryin, I'm gonna get you a Monte Carlo, didn't ya hear me? Didn't ya? Shhhhhh. Be quiet, your mum is tryin to sleep, okay? Shhhhhh! Come on. Come on. My little Danny boy baby. Come onnnn. Shhhhhhhh!

> *On the last "shhh" he has his hands around the baby's neck and he presses with the "shhh" too hard.*

Shhhhhh.

> *He looks at the baby. He is still as a lizard. Keeps looking at it and makes a sound of*

tasting with his mouth—tongue starts on roof of mouth, mouth opens, it ends up on bottom—about six times. Could be petit mal epilepsy. From now on his whole manner is extremely wooden, sort of like a mechanical man, trying to hide the fact. Looks at THERESA, *who is watching in wonder. Not sure what to do.*

It's okay. It's okay, it's not crying anymore. See, it's quiet now. It's not cryin. I—I done it—see? See? I'm a good father, he—you know how come he stopped? 'Cause I told him he was gonna get a Monte Carlo.

THERESA   What's that?

ALAN   It's a kind of car... *(as he's going out the door)* It's a place too. On one of them south sea islands... Maybe we'll go there, eh? I gotta go meet somebody... I'll see ya later...

> ALAN *goes.* THERESA *bursts into tears. She has been holding them in. She looks around, as if for someone to help her. Fingers in mouth. Puts her hand across her eyes and calls.*

THERESA   Danny? Danny? Beebee?

> *She slowly moves to it. Tiptoeing over, she looks in the crib and screams bloody murder. She picks it up and hugs it and falls to the ground.*

Oh my little beebee, my little darlin, what he done to you, what—what them marks all black and blue all over on your neck, he sttrangle you? He strangle you! Breathin. Breathin. *(She starts doing mouth-to-mouth.)* Come on baby, breathe! Come on, baby, don't let that bastard do this to ya! He's a bastard an we can beat him! *(looks at it)* Oh baby. Oh my baby little baby Jesus, you're goin with him now. Ahha. *(crying, kneeling)* Please. *(with baby swaddled up)* Hail Mary, full of grace, Lord is with ya. Blessed art thou amongst women and blessed is the fruit of thy womb, Jesus. Holy Mary, mother of God, pray for us sinners, now and at the hour of our death, amen. Dear God. *(crosses herself)* Take Danny with ya, please, he never done nothin to nobody, he jus a baby. He jus a baby. He jus a little baby.

She reaches for the phone.

Judith Thompson is a two-time winner of the Governor General's Literary Award for *White Biting Dog* and *The Other Side of the Dark*. In 2006 she was invested as an Officer in the Order of Canada and in 2008 she was awarded the prestigious Susan Smith Blackburn Prize for her play *Palace of the End*. Judith is a professor of drama at the University of Guelph and lives with her husband and five children in Toronto.